W9-AHM-997

Excellent Catholic Parishes

Excellent ✦

✦ Catholic

Parishes ✦

The Guide to
Best Places and Practices

Paul Wilkes

PAULIST PRESS
New York • Mahwah, N.J.

Jacket, cover and book design by Cynthia Dunne

Copyright © 2001 by Paul Wilkes

All rights reserved. No part of this book may be reproduced or transmitted in any form or by any means, electronic or mechanical, including photocopying, recording or by any information storage and retrieval system without permission in writing from the Publisher.

Library of Congress Cataloging-in-Publication Data

Wilkes, Paul, 1938–
Excellent Catholic parishes: the guide to best places and practices / by Paul Wilkes.
    p. cm
  Includes index.
  ISBN 0-8091-3992-8 (alk. paper); 0-8091-0529-2 (cloth)
  1. Parishes—United States—Case Studies. 2. Catholic Church—United States—Case studies. 3. Pastoral theology—United States—Case studies. 4. Pastoral theology—Catholic Church—Case studies.
I. Title
BX1407.P3 W55 2001
282'.73—dc21   00-051488
                                              CIP

Published by Paulist Press
997 Macarthur Boulevard
Mahwah, New Jersey 07430

www.paulistpress.com

Printed and bound in the
United States of America

Contents

Our Lady Help of Christians is a sterling example that new wine can be poured into an older wineskin. This venerable church was shabby and ill attended; now it is the vital center for activities for everyone from kids to Generation X to seniors. The staff has a common vision, yet is feisty enough to dissent.

St. Pius X takes the rich Latino spirituality and blends it with a Vatican II consciousness. Some thirty ministries work with the various communities within the parish; poor and middle-class Latinos worship and serve side by side. With strong community presence, this parish is the anchor for a changing neighborhood.

The Catholic Area Parishes have instilled hope in this farming area and demonstrated the value of cooperation. Five parishes pool their resources into a cluster ministry; three nuns and two priests are all pastoral leaders. Worship on Sunday is taken onto Main Street on Monday; gospel values come alive in small-town America.

The Catholic variation on the Willow Creek megachurch, Holy Family has ten thousand parishioners, one priest, but incredible lay participation. A big church is broken down into "communities" of ministries, ministries that cover everything from first-rate counseling to discovering needs people don't even realize they have. Family-conscious ministries and relevant homilies link faith to life.

5.   St. Peter Claver   ✦   73

New Orleans, Louisiana

St. Peter Claver changed the city's most dangerous neighborhood into one of the safest. Here is church-based community organizing at its best. Liturgy is deeply Catholic and deeply African American—drums and rosaries both are in use. An excellent school serves children of poverty. Parishioners have come into their own because of their involvement in a parish that sees its work as the total transformation of people and their community.

6.   St. Francis of Assisi   ✦   93

Portland, Oregon

Saint Francis of Assisi is a look into the future of the Catholic parish. It is headed by the mother of six children, a single parent. This is social justice, up close, with a wonderfully warm soup kitchen and multiple services for the poor. St. Francis is willing to live the "messy Word" of the gospels. Lay ownership is evident in this priestless, but powerful parish. There is strong emphasis (à la St. Francis) on the environment, namely a park for the homeless. Lay-driven, innovative liturgies draw people from miles around.

7. St. Francis of Assisi ✦ 109

Wichita, Kansas

At St. Francis of Assisi, every child is assured a free Catholic education, for tithing is at the heart of this church. But time and talent are rendered first, before treasure is asked for. A deep and reflective spirituality for parishioners has been engendered by thirteen years of round-the-clock eucharistic adoration.

8. St. Mark's ✦ 129

Boise, Idaho

The Life Teen Mass at St. Mark's reaches teenagers and transforms their lives. Twice-yearly evangelization retreats and then incorporation into small faith communities prevent people from getting lost at this vibrant parish. The power of faith stories sends people into the world knowing they are not alone in their struggles. What is most heartening is that lay people have actually formed their priests.

Introduction

If a person—either clergy or lay—were about to be assigned to a Catholic parish and could take only one book, I hope this is the one book that person would bring along. Call it a survival guide; call it a pattern for a successful parish. *Excellent Catholic Parishes* attempts to show both *what* a group of the most outstanding and inspiring parishes in America is doing and *how* successful approaches and programs can be replicated.

Excellent Catholic Parishes came into being after I returned from a parish in New Jersey where I had given a three-day pre-Lenten mission. Simply put: I loved being there. It was so alive; the parishioners and staff were so friendly and so ready to say "yes." The programs were varied and useful—both old and young were being educated, and people in their twenties were crowding into the Sunday night liturgy. Only when I returned to my home parish and a certain sadness came over me did I realize the dramatic difference between that parish and my own.

There were surely other parishes like that one in New Jersey, I assumed, and over the next two years, with the generous support of a grant from the Lilly Endowment, I and two researchers set out to find them.

We asked experts in parish renewal, we asked Catholic newspaper editors, we asked those who specialized in the various kinds of parishes—rural, Hispanic or those without a resident priest, for instance—to recommend the very best parishes they knew. Our list grew and grew. An index at the back of this book lists over three hundred of these exemplary parishes and often provides a capsule summary of what it is they do so well.*

Of those hundreds of parishes, I profiled eight to represent the various types from across the country. Within a short but detailed picture of each, I have highlighted three aspects of that parish's life that are exceptional but, more importantly, *reproducible*.

This book has two aims: to show that great parishes not only exist, they abound, and to illustrate that their

---

* A companion volume, *Excellent Protestant Congregations*, published by Westminster John Knox, tells of our search for excellent Protestant churches.

approaches to the various aspects of parish life can succeed elsewhere. As the reader will discover, neither these parishes nor their pastors are cut from some magical cloth that inured them from the problems facing both the Church and people today. In fact, these problems often made these parishes into the great places they have become.

I have tried to make the book easy to use. Indeed, like a survival guide, if a certain need presents itself, a ready answer is available. Those answers are encapsulated in the "points of excellence" highlighted at the beginning of each parish profile. An addendum contains still other "points of excellence." Quite frankly, the researchers—Marty Minchin and Melanie Bruce—and I found many successful approaches we wanted to include, some of which did not fit neatly into our parish-by-parish format. All aspects of parish life—from finances to devotions, social action to renovations, adult education to outreach to the unchurched—are covered. We also hope these "points of excellence" might someday be seen in thousands, not hundreds, of parishes.

This is just the beginning. A Web site (www.pastoralsummit.org) both allows a short, pictorial visit to the eight parishes and lists all the wonderful parishes we have found, so that anyone seeking a great parish can easily find one. If the book serves as a survival guide for those who work in parishes, I hope it also proves to be a survival guide for those seeking a parish home.

One can find many new approaches to spirituality and belief these days, but the parish remains the place most Catholics go for sustenance. In fact, two-thirds of all American Catholics are registered parishioners, a varied lot, to be sure. While pluralistic in their beliefs and practices, they are actually not as polarized as one might think. They are looking for—albeit in many different ways—a transcendent connection to God and guidance for their life's journey, a place where they will be at once nurtured and prodded.

Simple Catholic affiliation is no longer enough. Catholics today seek not just to be on the rolls of an institution through which they can dispatch their religious obligations; they want a meaningful spiritual home. Melanie, Marty and I hope the pages that follow will help people find such homes. It is not that we have found *all* the great Catholic parishes in America but we have found *some* of them.

An advantage in our research and travels was that we were not *of the church*; we were *in the churches*. In other words, we had no ideological bias; we did not officially represent any diocese or group. We weren't social scientists assembling data. We were laypeople, interested (and hopefully skillful) observers of parish life. We sought excellence—and we found it in abundance.

✦ ✦ ✦

My deep gratitude to the Lilly Endowment and Chris Coble, program director (religion), for believing in and supporting this "search for excellence"; to

Kathleen Walsh, my editor at Paulist Press; and especially to Marty and Melanie, who brought their own excellence to our joint effort.

Our Lady Help of Christians

573 Washington Street
Newton, Massachusetts 02458-1494
(617) 527-7560
www.ourladys.com

✦ POINTS OF EXCELLENCE: ✦

1. Little Things Mean a Lot

2. Liturgical "Rounds"

3. A Staff with Common Vision, Yet Willing to Dissent

Most priests would look upon Father Walter Cuenin's new assignment, Our Lady Help of Christians, as their worst nightmare come true. A deadening mustard color shrouded the interior of the once grand church. Someone had covered the finely sculpted columns with faux marble paint. The crucifixion mural above the altar—in its day a magnificent paean to Christ's redeeming power—was besmirched with years of soot; the figures appeared lost in a heavy, polluted fog. The church's high school was poorly maintained and attended. Roofs leaked; the rectory was dingy; the collection was down. One of seven Catholic churches in Newton, Our Lady's was perhaps the most visible, its French Gothic tower looming over the Massachusetts Turnpike near Exit 17. Yet, there was talk of closing the whole business down.

The flaws were not only external. Our Lady's parish had an equally distressed interior life. When young couples approached the parish office about marriage, they were often interrogated instead of welcomed. "You just about had to show your gas bill to prove you lived within the parish boundaries," one long-time parishioner says, "and then pull out your checkbook as evidence you could afford it." Baptisms and funerals were handled the same way; a series of hoops to jump through rather than a welcoming hand extended at these important life-cycle moments, which occur for both churched and unchurched Catholics.

Newton, whose simple double-deckers, fourplexes and modest homes once housed Irish, Italian and French immigrants, was an area in transition. The town still retained some elements of the classic ethnic parish structure (in fact, one of Father Cuenin's mandates was to close and combine a smaller French parish into Our Lady's, once predominantly Italian). These days young, emigrating professionals and the educated offspring of those Italian immigrants make up a large proportion of the population.

Walter Cuenin also possessed a somewhat distressed past and an uneven record. One of the best and brightest Boston seminarians, he had been sent to Rome for studies and had earned a doctorate from the prestigious Pontifical Gregorian University. After some unfulfilling years on the archdiocesan tribunal as an ecclesial bureaucrat he finally, as an associate in a parish, had the opportunity to implement his Vatican II vision of a new, collaborative church. When a decidedly pre—Vatican II pastor was assigned to his church and began to stifle the initiatives in lay ministries, liturgy and youth work that he had begun, Father Cucnin faltered. "You taught the people to think *they* were in charge of the parish!" the chancery admonished. While spoken as an accusation of misconduct, it reflected exactly what Father Cuenin had tried to do.

Then forty years old, Walter Cuenin went into a tailspin, a personal and clerical mid-life crisis. He asked for a year's leave of absence. He worked as a travel agent (never having worked for pay, he was determined to prove to himself he could make at least fifty thousand dollars), spent hours in formal therapy and days and nights in searing self-reflection. He knew his forthright and progressive ways did not always fall in line with the Boston hierarchy. Could he go on as a priest and, if so, in this diocese?

At year's end, he had topped the fifty-thousand-dollar mark, discovered that some of his battles with church authority had their roots in his own Irish Catholic *mishigash* rather than in the principles of good leadership and servanthood and that, indeed, a Vatican II advocate such as himself could find a place in this church.

As the pastor of Our Lady's he would have the opportunity to forge that vision, but he knew he had to find and tread much more carefully the line between open defiance and quiet, covert innovation to create a people of God in Newton. Before him lay the greatest challenge of his priestly life. Walter Cuenin took a deep breath and eagerly set to work.

Father Walter Cuenin

His first job had nothing to do with doctrine or dogma. Before he did anything else, he had to completely reorient the parish attitude, its culture. He knew that success would require Our Lady's to present an entirely new face to the people of Newton, a good number of whom had either gone to other parishes or left the Church entirely. He gently—and not so gently—made it clear that staff who wanted to continue the old "jump through the hoops" approach would either change or go. Two curates soon left. Because of the size of the parish, he could have received a newly ordained priest, but knew he would have to take whomever the diocese assigned. It was a wild card he chose not to play. With the ever declining number of available Catholic clergy, one priest parishes would soon be the norm, and Father Cuenin chose not to create structures that would soon be obsolete.

Instead, he hired lay pastoral associates, consciously looking for competent women, because they would bring a much-needed feminine component to parish life. Soon he had a first-rate staff in place, including Mary Ellen Cocks, one of the first certified lay pastoral associates in Boston and a woman with an excellent reputation as both a decisive administrator and a compassionate consensus builder. He assigned her the difficult task of working with the parishioners of St. Jean l'Evangeliste, a nearby French parish that would have to be closed and folded into Our Lady's.

Another face also had to be changed, and this would take more than hiring or firing a few staff members.

Walter Cuenin, infused with the splendor of Roman churches and a native sense of beauty, refused to serve as pastor at such an uninspiring church.

Such a task, as any pastor of an aging church soon realizes, is daunting. The cost to restore Our Lady's, while at the same time adapting it to Vatican II needs and current city building codes, would run upward of two million dollars. While facing the reality that New England ranks lowest in terms of charitable donations of any section of the country and that Catholics nationally are among the least generous of any religious group, Father Cuenin set before his people a vision of a place of worship completely restored to its 1881 French Gothic glory.

"It's very difficult to give glory to our glorious God if you are surrounded by ugliness," he says. "A leaking roof had stained the walls, and the place was poorly lit. To be perfectly honest, it was a mess. There was no pride in the place."

We sit on the side porch of his rectory on a warm May afternoon and Father Cuenin, a Friar Tuck of a man with ample girth and soft eyes incongruously encased in a rugged, almost pugilistic face, wears a light jogging jacket, khakis and an open knit shirt. An unassuming man, he answers his phone, "This is Walter." While he abides by the edicts of an archdiocese with a national reputation for its conservative practices and hierarchical strictures, he hardly embodies the clerical imperative.

I have come to Our Lady on this weekend in May because it marks a triumph for Father Cuenin. Cardinal

✦ 1. LITTLE THINGS MEAN A LOT ✦

When Father Walter Cuenin began the revitalization of his parish, he concentrated on both major programs and new approaches, but always emphasized that the little, immediate deeds often mean the most. "My daughter is wheat-intolerant and so she can't take the eucharistic bread," says Margaret Hannah. "Other priests said, 'Well, bring what you want and I'll bless it when the child comes to the altar,—which is not the same as consecrating it into the body of Jesus Christ. Walter made sure there was a rice wafer on the plate when he said Mass." When Donald Laurie confessed that because the family had lived abroad his eleven-year-old daughter had not received first communion and would be embarrassed to be put in a class with seven-year olds, Father Cuenin arranged to meet privately with her. And then, after a few private sessions, he went to the Laurie home for that important first communion.

Law would preside at 6 P.M. Mass that Sunday night to celebrate the completion of the church's restoration. As I was finding out, Father Cuenin had not only restored a church, he had revived a parish spirit as well in both grand and small ways. He helped transform a classic, older parish, combining Old Church architecture and traditions with New Church innovations to forge a

Catholic community so popular that people drive from all parts of Boston to be part of it.

Perhaps Lisa Schraffa, a voluble thirty-four-year-old computer software salesperson, speaks to what best expresses the draw of Our Lady's. "Acceptance. Welcoming." I hear these and similar words over and over again.

"It was two days after my then-husband told me the marriage was over and I found myself in Father Cuenin's office bawling my eyes out," she tells me as we stand in front of the church after morning Mass. "I had been away from the Church for probably eight or nine years. But when my marriage ended I wanted to go back, back to something I knew as a child. I still had my issues with the Church because of its stand on women, divorce, birth control, abortion and plenty of other things, but somehow this was my true spiritual home. I'm into channeling and reincarnation and a lot of New Age stuff, but beneath it all is a strong Catholic core.

"Walter told me I was welcome here, that we are all broken people and that broken people are exactly who the Church is there for. And he was honest. 'I cannot imagine what you are going through right now,' he said. 'I want you to talk this over with another woman, because she will understand this better than I possibly can.' He hooked me up with Mary Ellen Cocks and she did understand and it marked the beginning of my return to the Church."

Lisa goes out daily into a technoscientific world in which Bill Gates—not God—might be regarded as the Supreme Being and where coworkers might chide her for her beliefs. "I need a place where I can belong, where I'm not considered so weird, a place where I am nurtured so I can go back into the workplace and show those folks that a belief in God can make the biggest difference in your life."

Lisa's sessions with Mary Ellen Cocks also led to the creation of one of the support groups that organically sprouted up to address the needs and desires of women parishioners who had suffered loss through such traumas as death, divorce and abortion. "My group is a place where I can talk over how my faith infuses my work life, how other people deal with their life problems, how you can be a doubting—and yet a believing—Catholic."

Our Lady's is an amazing parish, not only for the breadth of ages and types to which it appeals, but also for its openness to those whom some might consider outside the normal Catholic axis. Gays and lesbians, the divorced, those who had left the Church for a variety of reasons constantly and specifically hear that they are integral, not peripheral, members of this parish community. At a first-communion Mass I attend, Father Cuenin welcomed quite an ecumenical group.

Not only were some of the parents of the children lapsed Catholics or non-Catholics, but so also were many of their extended families and friends. "You come from many faith traditions," he says. "I invite you to make this your spiritual home for today." While not a blatant invitation to share in the Eucharist, it was

Cardinal Law's visit

certainly not the written or spoken warnings issued in too many Catholic churches that only Catholics, in the state of grace, could "receive"—and that sinful Catholics and non-Catholics were not welcome at the Lord's table.

When a black male Baptist minister and a white female Congregational minister married—and neither church proved big enough—Father Cuenin offered Our Lady's for the ceremony. As a dozen Protestant clergy gathered around the altar to say prayers over bread and wine before distributing communion, Father Cuenin stayed tactfully to the side. Protestant and Catholic theological understanding of the Eucharist differs, and Father Cuenin, though a man who may work the edges of acceptable practices, does not needlessly court chastisement.

As further evidence of Our Lady's ecumenism, a Jewish day school uses the top floor of the high school.

And when Agudas Achim Anshei Sfard down the street was desecrated with anti-Semitic graffiti, Father Cuenin led the congregants from his parish to the synagogue, where they encircled the building with their bodies and their love.

While Our Lady's embraces such modern innovations as women's support groups and the ecumenical exchange of pulpits with Protestants and Jews, it also continues older traditions such as a magnificent procession that has its roots centuries ago in Italian villages. Each June, a three-day festival is capped by a procession of Our Lady of Mount Carmel through the Newton streets—streets with red, white and green stripes proudly painted to honor this Italian patron saint. The statue is even carried right to the windows of shut ins so they might see both the Virgin's and their neighbors' faces. When the statue reaches the churchyard, a child dressed as an angel slides down a wire and showers the Virgin with rose petals. An explosion of fireworks marks the festival's end as Father Cuenin, a gold cope draped about his shoulders, beams over the thousands in attendance. Newton Italians, who had felt in recent years that Our Lady's at worst denigrated or at best ignored their traditions and ethnicity, appreciate and embrace the revival of this ancient rite.

Our Lady's equally honors and employs Old World piety and New Age approaches in responding to the unique needs of the different segments of the congregation. It is a varied congregation, including the Lisas and other young professionals at Our Lady's, transplants from other cities, the old Italians who have lived here for decades, and their children who either never left or have returned, largely because of the community feeling of Newton and this church.

What brings them all together are the Sunday liturgies, which Father Cuenin feels are Our Lady's spiritual center. "The rhythm of the Eucharist, gathering together in the Mass—this is so crucial for 99 percent of the people," he says. Music is tastefully done; oboes, French horns and a grand piano are common instruments. Father Cuenin is an excellent homilist, always trying to make scripture applicable to what his people have or will encounter in their everyday lives.

There is at once a high-church feel to the liturgy here and yet an old-style, almost revivalist warmth. Pastoral associate Sister Marie LaBollita walks up and down the aisles before each service, checking in on the status of people she knows, seeking out those faces new to her. It harkens back to the days when the pastor made rounds of his parish, but as so many of the parishioners work during the day and even late into the night, this proves the best time to make contact.

"You can be real here," says Margaret Hannah, a forty-seven-year-old mother of three. "There aren't pretenses; people are not put in roles." As eighty-year-old Dorothy Reese notes, "Women used to be the dusters and the cleaners; here they are an integral part of the Church and evident in leadership positions." Both women note that Sister Marie had proved this

✦ 2. LITURGICAL "ROUNDS" ✦

While the liturgy at Our Lady Help of Christians is a well-orchestrated service, a wonderful blend of excellent music, on-target, practical homilies and dignified ritual—and tailored to the dominant group that attends (more sedate at 4 P.M. on Saturday, open to the chaos and noise of babies at 10 A.M. on Sunday and zesty at 6 P.M. for the teenagers and Generation X)—it also presents an opportunity that the lay staff does not overlook. Staff members "work the crowd," checking in on people they know are going through rough times, welcoming newcomers, making a point to talk to those they haven't seen in church. "One couple came back for the celebration of our restoration just because I welcomed them when they were here two years ago," said Sister Marie. Just the tortured look on a woman's face prompted Mary Ellen Cocks to ask how she was doing. Her marriage was in extremis. After a few sessions with Mary Ellen and more with a recommended marriage counselor, the relationship was saved, in part because of that morning's intercession.

"realness"—while retaining a healthy sense of humor—by participating in a parish fashion show. She appeared in both the flowing habit and starched wimple of her order, the Sisters of Charity-Halifax, and in a long, black cotton dress and stylish knit sweater with a vividly patterned silk scarf at her neck. In fact, Sister Marie is wearing a similarly tasteful outfit that morning as she makes her rounds, blending in nicely with her congregation.

This church, while it continues to reinvent itself, does not hold on to innovations or procedures that no longer work or are no longer needed. The liturgy committee provides one example, for it had, frankly, become superfluous. "On our scrutiny Sunday for our Rite of Christian Initiation group, we split the readings into three parts, with musical interlude to break it up,...things like that," says Father Cuenin. "But what was radical not so many years ago is now normal. You don't have to bust down fences or feel you have to innovate for the sake of innovation every Sunday."

Personnel policies at Our Lady's mandate good salaries—contrary to the classic Catholic approach that expects laypeople to donate their services or, if offered a modest salary, to gratefully accept whatever might be apportioned and then feel vaguely guilty about getting paid at all. "If you want professional help, you pay for it and pay well," says Father Cuenin. All parish staff receives and is expected to take four weeks' vacation. Each is budgeted for a conference or workshop at least yearly. And the most prestigious jobs—like supervising seminarian interns—are not all reserved for the pastor.

When Father Cuenin arrived, not only was the church in sad shape, so was the rectory. As is typical, it combined work and living areas, which was something he could not and would not tolerate. "How can you have a place with Gestetner forms stacked in the corners, Mass cards on the table and bulletins on the radiators and expect it to be a home you want to come back to?" He moved office functions to a parish center, modernized the rectory kitchen and hung pictures from his travels as well as newly purchased prints by Botticelli, Michelangelo and other masters throughout the rectory. Now home to Father Cuenin and four other priests in residence—none of whom serve at Our Lady's—the rectory is considered a model of fraternity throughout the archdiocese.

Father Cuenin, while in some ways a prototypical results-oriented church leader, realizes that certain things take time. He believed in his youth minister, Lawrence Molloy, even though Molloy's first two years didn't yield great results and only a modest number of teenagers got involved in the youth program. This year, his patience paid off. A work project, helping to build a home in Portsmouth, Ohio, drew kids like sixteen-year-old Jimmy Duffy. "I hated God; I felt I was being forced. I didn't want to know about all this church stuff," says Jimmy, a tall, thin boy with a ready smile. "But I saw the face of God in those faces on the project. They were so grateful we had come to help them. It turned me around. I love to be at church now." Another boy, diagnosed as bipolar, and a girl with a tough-as-nails reputation are two among many teenage lives that Our Lady's has touched. Thirty-two kids have signed up for the next work project, paying their own expenses to help out a family less fortunate than their own.

There is a sense that people quite simply *like* to be at Our Lady's—from sixteen-year-old Jimmy to thirty-four-year-old single again Lisa to forty-seven-year-old mother with young children Margaret to the eighty-year-old widowed Dorothy. While visiting there, I was reminded of the words of Peter Maurin, a cofounder with Dorothy Day of the Catholic Worker movement, for Our Lady's is a place where "it is easy to be good."

I feel that sense of belonging and enjoyment on the Sunday night Cardinal Law arrives to celebrate the successful restoration of Our Lady's. There is none of the false hilarity that too often passes for camaraderie in churches; instead, I sense a quiet confidence that indeed these are people about a serious and yet enjoyable task. While the parish customarily uses a Canadian inclusive-language lectionary, which is not formally authorized for use in the United States, they have brought out the authorized version for the cardinal's visit. A few rabbis, Protestant ministers and the Jewish mayor of Newton are also in attendance.

Cardinal Law starts off thanking the people and Father Cuenin for the magnificent restoration. "Some people think Walter is a liberal, but I know him to be hierarchical in the way he got this job done," the cardinal says with a smile. The first part, while perhaps not meant as a compliment, certainly could be taken as such, and the second, an attempt to synchronize

Father Cuenin's and the cardinal's own vision of the church, stretched the point considerably. But it didn't matter. The church interior looked magnificent: gold leaf adorned the columns, the crucifixion mural was now a vivid statement and the soft mauve-painted walls both restful and reverential. Outside, new slate glistened dully in the fading light; the towering steeple and its gilded cross beamed out over Newton.

The cardinal's sermon points out that while the church looked beautiful, it was not really the church at all. They, the people, were the church, the "living stones" called to infuse the world with their deep spirituality.

Mary Ellen Cocks focuses on those words. The parish had just completed a new survey, and while many had given Our Lady's high marks for inclusion, liturgy and welcoming, a commanding number of people wanted more emphasis on spirituality. They wanted retreats, spiritual speakers, Bible study and small groups. Our Lady's certainly could improve in that area, and no one knew that better than Mary Ellen. Now she had more fuel for the next staff meeting. Being collaborative never precludes any member of the Our Lady staff from pointing out where the parish needed to change, improve or even take an entirely new approach. This would be the first item on her agenda on Wednesday when they next would meet.

✦ 3. A STAFF WITH COMMON VISION, YET WILLING TO DISSENT ✦

Although staff members agree on a basic approach to parish life, opinions contrary to the accepted ways—while not always welcomed because of the changes or additional work they might entail—are at best encouraged or, at a minimum, tolerated. Each member of the team, from Father Cuenin on down, realizes they have their short suits and tries to listen when another member points out an area needing attention. "Spirituality is one of these areas," says Mary Ellen Cocks. Father Cuenin believes that the liturgy is the primary source of spirituality for "99 percent" of the congregation. His staff does not necessarily agree, feeling that many parishioners want a deeper, more contemplative spirituality. At least with this difference of opinion and emphases on the table—and occasionally returned to the table—Our Lady's will continue to do its best to meet the deepest needs of its people. "We do very well by *a* ruler," says Mary Ellen. "We have to strive to do well by *the* ruler."

St. Pius X

1050 N. Clark Road
El Paso, Texas 79905
(915) 772-3226
www.elpasoparishes.org/stpiusx.htm

✦　POINTS OF EXCELLENCE:　✦

1. Training Lay Leaders—Creating a Lay Institute

2. Evangelizing: Steps to Greater Lay Involvement

3. Choir as Community

The sun slips behind the imposing bank buildings and high-rise hotels that flank Interstate 10, busy now with the beginning of afternoon rush-hour traffic. The last of its blazing shards, streaming across a broad expanse of plaza just a few blocks away, strikes and sets ablaze a bronze statue of Jesus Christ. It depicts not one of the usual images of Christ, the triumphant savior or the bleeding crucified one, but the peasant Christ, with a rough-woven serape over his shoulders, a walking stick in one hand, a small bag in the other. It seems an anomaly here in this quiet sanctuary, yet so close to the world of commerce and the bustling Bassett Center Mall.

As Father Arturo J. Bañuelas stands beneath this at-once unassuming and imposing figure, the soft sounds of tumbling water from a three-tier fountain impart a sure peace to the place. Behind him sits the stately, mission-style stucco church of St. Pius X, now burnished to gold by the setting Texas sun.

"El Paso is a border town—between the United States and Mexico," he begins. "Hispanics are on the borders of the Anglo world; to be a Catholic is to stand at the edge of a secular society. Even today, the Church is still on the border between old ways and new ways, the traditional Church of Sunday devotion versus the Church that we carry into the world each day. So, it was appropriate that our 'Border Christ' would be the symbol of our church—always on the move, not ever at home, willing to go where he is needed, wearing the simplest of clothes, carrying no more than he needed but, because of his marginalized status, capable of entering all cultures and bridging all people as one."

Father Bañuelas's modest assessment of his parish and its signature statue belie what has happened here. St. Pius X has wedded ancient Hispanic values and

faith with a Vatican II vision of a modern parish, infusing each with new meaning. St. Pius X—or San Pio X
to its largely bilingual congregation—is considered
not only one of the most outstanding Hispanic
parishes in America, but one of the best, *period*. With
hundreds of its members solidly trained as lay leaders,
new ministries springing up virtually weekly and liturgies that appeal to everyone from *los jovenes* to *los
majores de edad*, this parish indeed serves as a ray of
hope for Hispanics (the fastest growing segment of the
Catholic America) as well as for the Church at large.

As I spend time at St. Pius, talk to parishioners and
witness some of their thirty-nine different ministries,
it quickly becomes clear that this parish has thrived for
two primary reasons. The first is the positive, willing-
to-risk attitude of its pastor. The second is a concerted
lay training program based both in periodic parish
evangelization retreats that lead people into small
Christian communities ("Among other things, they
make true Christians out of Sunday Catholics," one
person observes), and Tepeyac, a comprehensive lay
institute that provides theological formation for ministry. Good intentions and good ideas usually receive a
let's-try-it-and-see response from Father Bañuelas,
but not before the new ministers receive grounding
both in the teachings of their faith and the demands of
their new quest.

St. Pius has a visionary pastor in Father Bañuelas—
who received his Ph.D. from the Pontifical Gregorian
University in Rome—but it owes much of its success

✦ 1. TRAINING LAY LEADERS — CREATING A LAY INSTITUTE: ✦

Returning to the United States from his excellent education at Rome's Gregorian University, Father Arturo Bañuelas soon realized that if laypeople were truly to live out Vatican II's mandate to be "the priesthood of believers" they would need training. He began to hold weekend and summer courses for laypeople in theology, Christology and the Church's social documents under the umbrella of a newly formed Tepeyac Institute, named after the mountain at Guadalupe where the Blessed Virgin appeared to Juan Diego. The courses, while rigorous, were specifically geared to laypeople, so that they could better and more fully function in their various parish ministries. Since its founding, it has educated some 11,000 people, making it one of the largest diocesan lay institutes in America. "What happens is that people can have a common language and a common vision about their ministry," says Father Bañuelas. "They know the underpinnings; they can talk about it openly and intelligently. And then live it out."

to its laypeople. At St. Pius, laypeople are not considered "volunteers" in the programs they either originate or join; they are "ministers." They take literally the Second Vatican Council's mandate to become "collaborators in the priesthood of Christ."

One can see even from just a handful of St. Pius ministries—*Jovenes en Cristo*, Living Word Ministry, the Arms of Love AIDS ministry, the Personal Enrichment ministry, Singles in Mission and the *Colonia* ministry—that the parish not only penetrates the lives of its people, but also reaches beyond its comfortable borders as well.

As I sit with a group of *Jovenes en Cristo* members, they tell me how they came into being. As Hispanic Generation Ñ (the counterpart to the Anglo Generation X), they were too old for teenage activities and younger than the thirty-five-plus group. "We had no place to turn for guidance as we face some of the biggest decisions of our lives, decisions that will shape our lives," says Victor Hugo Arquelles, a handsome twenty-seven-year-old who owns a truck-repair business. They wanted the Church's guidance, and they craved good friends and fellowship.

While Father Bañuelas emphasizes such community building in everything from the "Tamales and Menudo" breakfasts after Sunday liturgies to the many fiestas staged on the plaza, he draws a line: "Community without service is a self-help group." So, while *Jovenes en Cristo* is a young-singles group, it is other-directed —playing bingo with kids with cancer in a hospital or taking fifteen at-risk teenagers on a retreat. When they do go out, they do so as an extended family, although none of them is related. After a night of dancing at a local club, Marisol Hernandez, a recent college graduate, says, "I came home after having a great time, but I felt so . . . so . . . pure. It wasn't the typical singles scene at all. I could hardly sleep, I felt so wonderful after being out with them."

Another group at St. Pius, which eventually came to be known as the Living Word Ministry, started with the passion drama that the parish stages each year on Good Friday. "Most of us had gone to Catholic schools, but we never saw the link between what we learned and what could be done with it," says Tom Chavez, who plays Jesus in the passion drama. "But after we all went to Tepeyac for classes, we saw that the passion drama was just a beginning; we could do so much more to make the gospels, the personalities in the Church come alive."

The group is now working on peace-and-justice dramas and plays that will feature the martyrs of the Americas. They even convinced Father Bañuelas—no televangelist, he—to allow them to record some of his sermons and sell them as a fund-raiser. "This is not a church in which you find hurdles," says Tom Chavez. "It is a church that takes you from your spiritual infancy and, with richer and richer protein, allows you to grow quickly and well."

The Arms of Love AIDS ministry began when someone in the church found out about an HIV-positive man named Jim, whom everyone had abandoned. Nothing was being done, spiritually, for AIDS victims in El Paso, but after Marta Huerta told Jim's story, relating how he'd cried tears of thanks because "nobody had hugged me for five years," a new ministry was born. When Marta and I visit a retired Army physician with AIDS in the hospital, I can see how strong her love is and how deeply she focuses on this man, who clearly returns the feeling.

At dinner with members of the Singles in Ministry group at a local restaurant, I am impressed with their concern for one another and their ability to go out and have a great time while still maintaining a strong focus on the need to serve. Stella Dominquez owns her own business, selling woodworking machinery in Mexico; Mary Durandt is a CPA; Berta Molina, a Headstart teacher; Carolina Del Rio works with abused children; and Pete Galvan, who is raising his son as a single parent, works as a school security guard. They all have comfortable lives, yet in their group they find both family and a vehicle to help them reach out. At Christmas, this group gathers hundreds of sweaters, coats and blankets for their sister parish in Juarez, Mexico, and during the year they organize and host personal growth workshops for singles who search, as they once did, for meaning in their lives.

"Like the Eucharist, as single people or divorced people, our lives are broken," says Pete, showing keen theological insight and not a trace of self-pity. "Christ shared his brokenness with us, so we must share ours with others, in service."

One might expect to hear such words from ordained clergy, but coming from the mouth of a

Father Arturo Bañuelas

layman? What continually impresses me as I talk with these people across such a wide spectrum of interests and ages is the theological depth and the organic quality of the St. Pius ministries. They had risen up out of the human needs of the parishioners and out of a desire to extend themselves into the world. This parish had helped them begin. Father Bañuelas had focused those needs, directing them at once inward and outward.

It is not that all of these people had been faithful Catholics and active parishioners before they experienced the liberating possibilities of St. Pius. Many had fallen away from the Church, finding their local parishes neither encouraging of their dreams nor spiritually nurturing. Some had had bad experiences with the Church that prompted them to leave. Today, it is not uncommon for St. Pius parishioners to pass two or three Catholic parishes to come here; some travel as many as fifteen miles.

Fernie Anchondo had been raised in a Catholic home but had strayed from his roots. He had married—though not in the Church—and now had a young daughter. "I knew my life wasn't what it should be," says Fernie, a man with a glistening, shaved head and smiling eyes, "and I wanted to go to confession. The priest wouldn't even hear my confession because I was outside the Church. I found Father Arturo and I confessed to him and the dam burst. I cried as I never cried before, but Father Arturo has the ability to make the path back to the Church seem easy, natural. He said I should ask my wife if she would marry me in the Church. She was overjoyed and we had our wedding at St. Pius X. It was beautiful and the beginning of a whole new life for us."

When a member of the St. Pius X group scheduled to travel to Mesa, Arizona, for a Life Teen workshop could not go, Fernie was asked to fill in. "It changed my life again; I saw what could be done for teenagers, how the faith could come alive. But we were not rich and white like the Mesa church; we had to adapt it for our kids." He now coordinates the Life Teen ministry, and Ashley, his nine-year-old daughter, and wife, Veronica, also actively participate. Life Teen is one of St. Pius X's most vibrant ministries and draws teenagers from all parts of El Paso. "My house is not my home," says Fernie. "This church is my home."

For Frank Lopez, who had also for a time left the Catholic Church in search of a deeper spiritual encounter with God, the prospects of a lucrative legal practice and a comfortable upper-middle-class life faced off against the gospel values that St. Pius X espouses and practices. "And the gospel finally and clearly spoke to me," he says. A graduate of the prestigious University of California-Berkeley Law School, Frank could certainly have joined an upscale law firm. Instead, he took a position with the University of Texas-El Paso to work on the thorny issues of border law, and he has made a personal commitment to St. Pius X's sister parish, *Nuestra Señora de los Angeles,* which is a few miles from the church but at the same time is a world removed.

As Frank and I walk the dusty, unpaved streets of the *colonia* (simply, "neighborhood" in Mexico, but the word connotes a poor area in the United States) in Juarez, just across the border from El Paso, he shows both pride that St. Pius X could help, and humility, for he has not forgotten his roots. "My father emigrated from Mexico and only went to the sixth grade; we never had much, but in our house in El Paso immigrants constantly came through, and they were treated with respect and dignity. Our work here is not about charity, just about bringing food or clothes for the poor. It is a walk together with the people of the *colonia.* We visit them; they visit us. We might be able to provide medical supplies for their clinic or furniture and toys for the day care, but when they come to El Paso they bring their music and their faith. We need each other; after all, we are one family. My heart was always with the poor, but it was only after I studied the documents of Vatican II at Tepeyac that my intellectual needs were met. I saw the 'why' behind the 'what' that I wanted to do."

Luis Vega, who lives in Juarez and who cut back on his work as an engineer when the gospel spoke to his life, joins us on our walk. Each man could have had a comfortable life, but each gives a good part of himself to work here in the *colonia*. We tour the clinic, which provides excellent if simple birthing for mothers at only forty dollars, and the church building, innovatively bisected so that the back half could be made into a badly needed day care center. The pride the men take in "their" church is palpable.

After winding our way up the mountain through narrow, labyrinthine roads and squatters' encampments, we visit one of the satellite churches. It is constructed entirely of shipping pallets and, to keep out the wind, lined with a pale blue medical wrap from one of the American-owned *maquilas*, or factories, in Juarez. To the parishioners it is Chartres, for God dwells here. The people of St. Pius had come to visit this church not long before, so a sign still hung against that blue backdrop. "Welcome, Sister Parish," it proudly proclaimed.

In essence, people like Marta Huerta and Frank Lopez and Fernie are, although they might not know it, vowed religious of a new kind of lay order that as yet has no name. In a parish like St. Pius, with excellent religious formation, support and encouragement, they are able to live out their quite serious religious vocations while remaining in the secular world.

This is exactly where Father Bañuelas sees the church going. "I am a dinosaur," he says with a smile.

"Laypeople, in real and meaningful collaboration with a priest, are the future of the church. This is no quick fix. This is a long haul. And we need to make changes, especially for Hispanic Catholics. We are losing them to other churches, because in the Catholic Church, instead of honoring and utilizing their rich faith and heritage, we are still trying to assimilate them, make them into Eurocentric Catholics. They are not.

"What is this? You drape a serape over an altar and that is Hispanic culture; that is a Hispanic church? A serape is for your sofa." We are sitting at the kitchen table in the St. Pius X rectory, which sees a steady flow of parishioners and a busy schedule of meetings and activities. His passion is evident, yet his voice is controlled and even. "For Hispanic people, the priest is part of the family, and so my house is their house, as their houses are open to me. We must break down the barriers with the priest up here and the 'miserable' people down there. We have to take people's native intelligence and their passion, and our symbols—ah, the symbols are very important—and shape that into a new vision of a church, where the people are equals with the priests and the priests will lead, but they will always listen to the wisdom and the breadth of experience of the people. We must welcome them—that is what other churches are doing, and people flock to them—and not put up barricades."

I ask whether he thinks there is a priest shortage, and Father Bañuelas answers, "Yes and no. Yes, in that people might not be anointed before death by a priest, or a priest might not take the casket to the cemetery, or their classes might not be taught by a priest.

"No, there is no priest shortage, because the mission of the Church becomes more credible when laypeople

✦ 2. EVANGELIZING: STEPS TO GREATER LAY INVOLVEMENT ✦

In the weeks before one of St. Pius X's evangelization retreats, parishioners literally go door-to-door, fanning out into the neighborhood, inviting both stranger and parishioner alike to come. The retreat is also advertised in the bulletin and discussed from the pulpit. The evangelization retreat, which begins on Friday evening and goes through Sunday at noon, combines parishioners' stories of their own spiritual journeys (on such topics as sin, faith, conversion, discipleship), with liturgies, short talks by a priest and time for both group discussion and fellowship. The parish uses the SINE (*Sistema Integral de Nueva Evangelization*) approach, developed in Mexico City by Father Alfonso Navarro. After the retreat everyone who has come is contacted once a week for the next three weeks so that the "high" that often follows will not dissipate. Small Christian communities are formed. Active participation in parish ministries—or the beginning of a new ministry—naturally follows.

are also the leaders. When they evangelize, when my deacon Jim Szostek—who owns a pet shop—gives the sermon, when he has a statue of the Virgin in his store window in a shopping mall, those are a powerful witness to the world. Laypeople don't have the restrictions clergy do; they are everyplace. That is why this is a very creative time in the Church and a most exciting time to be a priest—dinosaur that I am—because the priesthood is multiplied time and time again out in the world by our parishioners.

"Some other parishes look upon us as radical, liberal, political, but we are not. We are theologically, liturgically solid, yet we adapt to people's needs. All that has happened here is that people have been given back their church, total possession—and they bring a unique Chicano flavor with it."

The way that Father Bañuelas has taken the native reverence for the Virgin of Guadeloupe and fashioned a Vatican II vision that swept the revered Virgin of the sixteenth century into the twenty-first serves as a tribute to the inculturated Catholicism he has shaped during his twelve years at St. Pius.

"What the Virgin—a woman of color, who embraces all cultures—tells us is that we are a universal people, a universal Church. There are no barriers of culture or race or status: Christ embraces us all and we, in turn, must embrace all, without prejudice. If the Virgin, this woman of color, is carrying the Christ Child, then for all Hispanics that is an affirmation: If the mother of Christ looks like us, then there must be a dignity to us.

This is not the Virgin of Lourdes or Fatima, forecasting the end of the world; this is the living Virgin that, while society might not accept you, accepts you, loves you, listens to you.

"But then, when we take the powerful social teachings of the Church, the vision of Vatican II, to evangelize the world, it moves from a personal piety to a faith that goes everywhere with us, calls on us to serve the poor, the sick, the lonely—both within our own circles and in the world at large. There is a unique mestizo spirituality and I believe it can really help the American Church to find itself in these confusing times. The wonderful thing about being Hispanic and working with mestizo spirituality is that we don't have to find our faith; we have faith. Regardless of what they have heard about their culture—as a boy I was discouraged from speaking Spanish, as were many others—in this parish we proclaim that what they have is good. The issue is how to inform that faith and deepen it."

On the Sunday I visit, deacon Jim Szostek preached. He handily moves from the gospel reading on Christ calling the disciples to be fishers of men to weave a fine homily, including both scriptural references and practical examples.

The Life Teen liturgy that evening, with the young associate pastor, Father Alejandro Reyes, presiding, is a festive, hand-clapping celebration containing an extraordinary gospel message—again based on that same scriptural passage. First, Father Reyes reads from want ads about qualifications for jobs, then four teenagers

St. Pius X, plaza

speak about their talents (beauty, intelligence, solid education) only to have the church grow dark and God's (actually Fernie Anchondo's) voice proclaim he needs everyone to work in the world and that qualifications mean little; faith and love are the measure. All could bring in the rich harvest of souls. The hundreds of teenagers and parents singing and holding their hands to heaven together creates a vivid impression; any parish in America would have gladly claimed them as its own.

When Father Bañuelas arrived, the parish had the nickname "Our Lady of the Highways"—a quick in-and-out location to dispatch an onerous obligation. The church building, as the pastor recalls, was "nothing more than a glorified gym." Today, the original church building serves as exactly that for the use of the parish and excellent parish school of 550 children, and a new church has been constructed. Space and gathering areas were crucially important, so the architects—in consultation with laypeople and Father Banuelas—designed three major gathering areas: a large gathering room indoors, a wraparound veranda and a sprawling plaza that speaks to the fiesta-prone, communitarian nature deep within Hispanic people. "So there are three places where people can gather before and after church," he says. "This is so important, that the people of God have a natural place to stop and to talk—about the Church, about their lives. Perhaps more gets accomplished in these places than in formal meeting rooms."

Indeed, as I stand in these places during my visit, I observe the Mexican village alive once more, *los jovenes* and *los majores de edad* mingle easily; few seem in a hurry to leave. It is time to catch up on one another's lives.

In addition to the content of the Tepeyac courses and the evangelization retreats, Father Bañuelas firmly believes that images also form souls. St. Pius X parishioners are continually reminded both of their heritage and their mandates. Sixteen stained-glass windows encircling the cupola of the new church depict a litany of the saints of the Americas—from Archbishop Oscar Romero, who was martyred in El Salvador for his outspoken defense of the poor, to Isaac Jogues, a legendary missionary, to Juan Diego, the humble peasant to whom *Nuestra Señora de Guadalupe* appeared in 1531. A statue of Jesus Christ, one hand summoning, the other sending forth, seems to float behind the altar, gazing out over the congregation.

As people leave the church, a stunning stained-glass window in the gathering area reminds them that their spiritual work, rather than ending, has just begun. Father Banuelas calls it "The Last Supper Yet to Come." All races come together, the saints of the ages sit with the workers of today, the lion and lamb rest together, alpha and omega are joined, different foods and animals from around the world abound. And, like all the stained glass at St. Pius X, it does not close out the world to form a holy, exclusive sanctuary. The colored glass is transparent, revealing the world beyond.

"I cannot say how important it is for people to have ambiance, to have symbols that speak to their experience," Father Bañuelas says. "We have simple needs, so it is basically a simple church, a space to be used, not only for liturgy, but for community events [a black Baptist choir performed to a packed house one night during my visit], to be visited whenever a person *stops by*. That is why we are open all day. Yes, things get stolen every once in a while, but to restrict people from visiting their home would just not be right. That is not what a church is for, just to be used on Sundays."

Throughout my visit, I hear stories of conversion at St. Pius X—not conversions to Catholicism, but *within* Catholicism. Small acts of kindness or encouragement by their pastor made the crucial difference.

✦ 3. Choir as Community ✦

Most of the St. Pius X choir does not know how to read music and many have never sung in a choir before, yet the eighty-voice choir is one of the finest in El Paso. "This is not only about rehearsals," says choir director Lisa Vasquez, who was not even a church going Catholic herself when a call intended for her father reached her. The pastor of St. Pius X wanted someone to start a choir. "I liked music, so I said, 'why not?'" After some 175 people showed up for auditions, a choir was quickly underway, but Lisa had something more in mind, quickly picking up on the parish's community spirit. "We cry together, pray together, go on special retreats together, celebrate birthdays, births, mourn deaths. There is something undefinable that comes out of a group that has shared so much together. It goes beyond our talents, our voices. Something else is at work."

Lisa Vasquez was an alienated Catholic when Father Banuelas asked her to help start a choir. Over 175 people came for auditions and now, years later, she leads one of El Paso's best. Julie and Gary Moore belonged to another parish when they were informed that their oldest daughter, Kelly, had a life-threatening medical condition. They called their parish, but their pastor was at dinner and could not be disturbed. A call to Father Arturo brought him to the hospital within the hour. Natalie, the Moore's youngest daughter, felt ambivalent about having a *quinceanera*, the sometimes expensive coming-of-age celebration for fifteen-year-old girls. But when Father Bañuelas, the Moore family and other members of the congregation traveled on pilgrimage to Guadalupe, he arranged to have one at the Virgin's basilica there.

One older woman tells me flatly, "Our pastor hasn't just changed a parish; he changed our lives." Missy Gonzalez, an attractive high school senior, comes up to me, looks at me through perfectly mascaraed eyes and says, "Father Arturo didn't teach me to be a Catholic; he taught me how to have a faith."

St. Pius X has simply brought out the best in people, tapped talents they didn't know existed and made Catholicism the moving force in their lives. As I sit amidst some of the parishioners in the rectory one afternoon, one of two hearing-impaired women, who had been included in the discussion through people signing to them, raises her hand. "Once you have a parish like this," she says with perfect diction, "you just won't have it any other way. When Father Arturo leaves, we will miss him badly, but something has begun here that will only get stronger."

Catholic Area Parishes

(Benson, DeGraff, Danvers, Clontarf and Murdock, Minnesota)

508 Thirteenth Street North
Benson, Minnesota 56215
(320) 842-4271
www.catholicareaparishes.org

✦ POINTS OF EXCELLENCE: ✦

1. Prepared to Participate at Weekly Liturgy

2. Cluster Ministries

3. Ministry of Presence

In those heady, storied days as the Upper Midwest was settled, both James J. Hill and John Ireland were giants. And while they left their mark in vastly different ways, they shared a common trait: each possessed a steely will. When these men wanted something to happen, they let nothing stand in their way. Hill ran a railroad, laying track relentlessly west. Ireland was a priest and later the bishop of St. Paul, Minnesota, determined to look after both the spiritual and temporal well-being of a burgeoning Catholic population. Two more unlikely collaborators are hard to imagine.

In the mid-nineteenth century Hill needed settlers to tame, populate and farm the land along his track line. He wanted to develop trade and commerce so that the St. Paul and Pacific Railroad had products and raw materials to ship and ready customers to buy them. Ireland looked east to the millions of Irish immigrants who had escaped the devastating potato famines to seek a better life. They had made it to these shores, only to founder in fetid urban slums. Protestant America had little use for their labor, their suspect Catholic religion that pledged allegiance to a foreign pope or their Old Country ways.

Hill wanted reliable, industrious people and Ireland had plenty of them, so the two men struck a deal. If Hill would make some 117,000 acres of railroad land available, Ireland would supply the farmers. And in each settlement along the rail line, he would found a Catholic church for these settlers and assure them a resident pastor to help these primitive communities develop into stable, productive towns.

In the late 1870s and early 1880s, tiny colonies sprung up out of the flatlands like so many well-spaced stalks of corn. The land was rich, flat and treeless. It proved ideal for farming, but a bit scant on lumber. Yet for prices as low as a dollar and a half an acre, it was a landless immigrant's dream. Benson, which became the Swift County seat, DeGraff, Danvers, Clontarf and Murdock were five of these new settlements.

For much of the next century the residents endured the vagaries of weather and market prices, but not until the further mechanization of farming, which required less labor and more capital, and the advent of large-scale agribusiness some twenty years ago did the hardest of times hit. More and more farmers were forced out of business. Population began to shrink. Stores, post offices and parish schools closed. *Consolidated* was the word used, but it simply meant the end of treasured parts of rural life, proud and independent as it was. *Consolidated* became a hated word, death in a mocking, polysyllabic disguise. At about the same time, oddly enough, dramatic changes took place in Catholicism, the faith that had sustained so many of these farmers. On a parallel track, priests and nuns left religious life. Population shifted; churches closed. So when their bishop (now in New Ulm, Minnesota, which split off from St. Paul in 1954) asked members of these five Minnesota towns to consolidate so that they might pool their resources and better utilize their staff, many saw it as another defeat, another imminent closing.

"Look, when we got word of this, I was ready to fight it to the death," says John Shekleton, the robust sixty-three-year-old owner of the Murdock Cafe, over a

breakfast of sausage, eggs and hash browns one morning after Mass. "Nobody was going to take my church
away from me, the church founded by the ancestors of
the townspeople who come in here every day."

That was twenty-two years ago.

"The way it worked out is simply amazing," his wife,
Roxanne, adds; "we really got the best of all worlds,
better programs, because we could do one well rather
than five half-baked, and have five pastors instead of
one."

Upon arriving at the Catholic Area Parishes' office
in Benson—the only one of the five towns appearing
on my map—and being greeted by Sister Clara Stang,
a Franciscan, it is obvious that Roxanne didn't exag-
gerate. Not only had the consolidation taken place, it
had succeeded and even provided the model for a new
kind of extended Catholic parish. I would learn that
while this heartland community had not been miracu-
lously transformed into the Woodstock nation, the
rugged individualism of rural America had given way
to the gentle communitarian gospel message.

The staff meeting on Wednesday mornings provides
just one example of a rare kind of ecclesial cooperation
and synergy. Here not only does the staff coordinate
programs for the one thousand families scattered across
some four hundred square miles, they also agree upon a
unified message for the coming weekend's liturgy. In
addition, they write up three points or questions, which
are included in each week's bulletin, to encourage
reflection on the next week's gospel reading.

Church of the Visitation, Danvers

This particular week focuses on Mark's story of Christ promising to refresh those who are weary and explaining that if they take up his yoke they will find it easy to carry. The questions are straightforward and practical: "Recall a burden made light by giving it to God." "Speak of how you were affected by a person who was strong in conviction but gentle in approach." "How do you let life make you weary?"

The homilists for the two Saturday-evening and three Sunday-morning liturgies would reflect upon and in some way address these points. They would also be used to focus discussion in the fifteen to twenty small faith communities that would gather that week and would be read at every parish meeting. Mark's story and those three points of departure would permeate those five Minnesota communities for an entire week. They would be confronted and hopefully lived out.

✦ 1. PREPARED TO PARTICIPATE AT WEEKLY LITURGY ✦

The Catholic Area Parishes in Minnesota don't wait for Saturday afternoon or Sunday morning to proclaim the weekly scripture readings to their parishioners. Instead, so that everyone in the five parishes is ready to actively participate in the weekend liturgies, the assigned readings are woven into the fabric of both parish and everyday life. Not only has the staff met and decided on a unified approach for the liturgies, they have made the readings an integral part of every meeting and gathering each of the five parishes will have that week. Whether the story of the loaves and fishes or the transfiguration, the theme is on parishioners' minds throughout the week. The fertile seed of the Word of God has an opportunity to sprout and be fruitful before people file into the pews.

"We are constantly working on unity here," says Father Steven Verhelst, the pastor of St. Francis in Benson. Father Ronald Huberty, pastor of Sacred Heart in Murdock, and pastoral administrators Sister Clara at the Church of the Visitation in Danvers, Sister Darlene Gutenkauf at St. Bridget's in DeGraff, and Sister Louise Bauer at St. Malachy's in Clontarf comprise the Catholic Area Parishes' leaders. "And, while I am the presider at the liturgy, it is the assembly that is important. They are the people of God; from this extended family comes the Spirit. And they need not be territorial; shared resources mean that everyone can benefit. And it has caught on. I've heard it over and over again from our parishioners: 'These used to be priests' parishes—now these are people's parishes.' That is a high compliment; that is ownership," Father Steve continues.

"We've learned a lot, made a lot of mistakes and hopefully gotten a few things right over the years," explains Sister Clara, who came here seven years ago. "While it isn't on the spiritual side of the ledger, when the parishes agreed to pay the staff out of a common budget, the people really voted with their dollars to be a community."

As Tim Mattheisen, who with his wife, Carol operates Do-Mats Supermarket, tells me over lunch at the Benson Subway shop, "We all knew one another, but that didn't mean we necessarily were praying as a community or really befriending one another. The singing, the liturgy, really gets me going." Not a man to swoon in spiritual ecstasy, he said, "I feel like leaping into the air when I leave church. I do. I actually do. Something is happening here, and we all can feel it."

This consortium of parishes—perhaps the first in the country—has carefully used the strengths of each member of the pastoral team and yet allows each parish to maintain its individual identity. Sister Darlene is a talented musician and liturgist who also

✦ 2. CLUSTER MINISTRIES ✦

"Our churches were just too small, the priest shortage was apparent; everyone was stretched trying to do too many jobs—and quite frankly, everyone having 'their' parish wasn't working; we weren't offering the best to our people," says Sister Clara Stang. When five Minnesota rural parishes banded together over twenty years ago, it was considered a revolutionary idea, not only for clergy to cooperate in this way, but for individual parishes to be served by someone other than "their" priest. "The important thing that we always stress is that each parish still does have a pastor or— in the case of women religious like myself—a pastoral administrator, but that each parish gets the best-qualified person in the various areas of church life. Farmers know about specialization; there are very few farms that have a few chickens, a few hogs and a cow. Specialization works; there are advantages to having a class of fifteen kids versus five classes of three kids apiece."

enjoys working with the elderly. Sister Louise has a gift for teaching children and young people in religious education. Sister Clara is considered a proficient organizer and a visionary; she works intensely with small faith communities. Father Ron is the RCIA expert and a compassionate listener, an excellent counselor. Father Steve is good with youth, liturgy and administration. So that no one assumes that "father" has a more important role than "sister" in these five parishes, both priests and nuns receive the same salary.

The churches combine for liturgical planning and RCIA preparation as well as share a religious education curriculum. The small Christian communities cross parish lines, but each parish still has its own parish council, finance and education committees, holds religious education classes in the parish and controls the funds directly related to that church's upkeep and specific needs.

The area parishes also come with demands. "That was pretty wimpy," Sister Darlene or Father Steve might respond to a poorly sung hymn in practice or even during a liturgy. They expect more feeling, more gusto and more volume when it is repeated. If food is needed for a reception after a funeral or if a committee or council needs members, the staff is hardly shy about making those needs known.

The parish does not request, it *requires* a high level of lay participation and leadership. "Everybody has to pitch in; you can't hide in these little towns," Roxanne Shekleton says, laughing. "In order to keep it all going, you are on a number of committees, teaching, baking, cleaning, doing something for one or more of the churches."

Traveling the miles of lonesome roads that join these five churches and five rectories, I am struck with the lush beauty of this part of the country. Rows of soybean plants and corn stalks stretch to a horizon uncluttered by buildings. In each town, a towering grain elevator and the steeple of the Catholic church remind anyone passing through exactly what goes on here.

Sitting in living rooms and local gathering spots, walking through dusty farmyards and attending an afternoon Good Harvest Mass, I am also struck by the unfettered sincerity and honesty of the people. Although farmers now rely on huge tractors to pull eight-row corn choppers instead of using a horse to pull a single-row plow, the pioneer stock endures. They have access to the Internet, satellite dishes and all the siren songs of the outside world, but there is a palpable centeredness to these rural people.

"Sometimes it seems like America has forgotten us," says Nancy O'Leary, the area parishes' bookkeeper. "But in certain ways that's exactly what we want. I think we have a sense of community out here that everybody could learn something from."

"People are crying out for meaning in an era of fragmentation," observes Father Steve, "and rural people are beautiful examples of living a meaningful life. But their way of life is constantly being threatened. These people have tremendous pressures upon them, yet they have so much to teach us."

These Catholics and their parishes in five tiny towns at the edge of the prairie have benefited both institutionally and personally from their consolidation. The parishes have anchored these people through some tough and stormy days. When others left, the churches stayed—and not only stayed, but prospered.

Each parish has placed an emphasis on instilling a sense of community and providing a place for people to gather. The Benson parish raised a million dollars to build a gorgeous receiving area at the front of the church; Murdock also built a new gathering space. DeGraff, Danvers and Clontarf removed benches at the back of the church to open them up.

Stories of conversion, like Kevin McGeary's, abound. I visited with Kevin in his modest farmhouse overlooking four hundred acres of family land he can no longer profitably farm. He had to rent out the land and now earns his living driving a grain truck. The past two decades have proven difficult in many ways for young men like Kevin, as the pensive and sometimes pained look on his face readily shows.

"I got into drugs in the service, drank too much when I got back, eventually got divorced and was generally messing up my life," he begins as we sit at his kitchen table. Sister Clara listens, but says nothing. "But Sister helped me get an annulment, let me see I was not only worthy to receive the Eucharist, but that Christ really wanted to feed me. Then she hooked me up with an ATEC (Adults and Teens Encounter Christ) retreat, which was the best weekend of my life; it really turned me around. I saw what my life was about: to spread Jesus' Word and his love. Jesus became my high. Now, Visitation is my family, my

*Sister Louise Bauer,
Paul Wilkes,
Sister Clara Stang*

gathering place, instead of some bar or liquor store. This is my home." Once a "Sunday Catholic—at best" who felt exiled by the Church, now Kevin McGeary has become one of Danvers' most active members, a leader in the RENEW program the parishes were preparing to launch.

Over his table hangs a reproduction of Thomas Blackshear's painting, *Forgiven*, a painting of Christ holding an exhausted worker, mallet in hand, in his arms. "I know the feeling," he says.

As Sister Clara and I drive back to the Danvers rectory where she lives, I glance over at her. She gives quiet testimony to what new and powerful roles religious women play in a changing Church. Straightforward, not pious, she radiates a deep spirituality. In essence, she reflects the best of Minnesota farmers: she takes less than she gives, works hard and persistently, and never calls attention to herself. She is a superb pastor.

Sister Clara takes children, parents and adults through the steps leading to the sacraments of baptism and reconciliation, yet she must step aside as a priest performs the rites. She has been a powerful presence in Kevin's and many other lives, and she awaits the time when her Church will allow her to do still more.

"I don't think we're any kind of ideal Catholics," says John Shekleton, "but these people (Father Ron is sitting across the table from him, representing the team) have helped us to have a little more charity, to open up, to be able to talk about religion as a part of life. That if we *don't* take what we hear on Sunday into Monday, we've missed the point."

He recalls the death and funeral of Willie Schwendermann, a Murdock resident hardly beloved for his irascibility and tendency to fight with almost anyone over just about anything. "Willie was harvesting sunflowers and had a heart attack. He had a big squabble just the night before. But when he went down on his knees alongside his pickup that day, I just know he made it right."

John Kelly, who owns McGovern's Grocery, is a man whose ever smiling face conceals the soul of a very private, Midwest stoic. "I have a tough time opening up, but you know, when you get to know people from the inside, not just what you see on the surface, most of 'em are pretty great."

Sisters Clara, Darlene and Louise and Fathers Steve and Ron are woven into the lives of these communities. They do their counseling in kitchens and on street corners, in barnyards and parking lots. Father Steve serves as the president of the Benson Chamber of Commerce. "We never saw a priest in the coffee shop in the old days," says John Shekleton. During the time I spent in Minnesota none of the staff wore clerical garb, except priests on the altar.

The community spirit spills over into the various tasks that face any parish. For instance, on designated Sunday mornings twice a year, parishioners show up at Visitation in Danvers in work clothes, towing backhoes and riding mowers behind their vehicles. After Mass, they clean the rain gutters, trim the trees and thoroughly clean all the buildings.

"Out here we are believers in what my grandfather from Belgium used to say: 'The grass is always greener where you water it,'" explains Father Steve. "We take what we have and try to make these parishes into the great places that they can be." For example, Sister Clara works with farm wives who put out the quarterly *Farm Women News*, as well as with a group that writes and stages plays that are both hilarious and perceptive about the role of women in rural life.

The five Minnesota parishes, however, hardly comprise some perfect Catholic world, free of jealousy, hate and selfishness. When representatives of a Hmong

✦ 3. MINISTRY OF PRESENCE ✦

Rarely does either of the priests of the Minnesota Cluster wear his Roman collar in public. The three sisters wear a small cross and pretty much anything they choose. "Look, everyone in this town knows I'm a Catholic priest," says Father Steven Verhelst. "But somehow when I'm in a shirt collar just like the rest of the folks here, it may not break down barriers, but it sure doesn't put any up." They visit farms and walk into the local stores, have lunch in the restaurants. "Some of the best things happen when you're standing in the kitchen with a woman making supper or out in the barn with her husband as he's fixing a tractor," says Sister Darlene Gutenkauf. "We are people; they are people. We want to prove we are not some sort of rare breed, and the best way is to do that the way the Lord did it, just by being with the people in the everyday experiences of their lives."

community from the Twin Cities explored the possibility of resettling some of their people in the Benson area to work at a clothing manufacturing firm, negative comments from townspeople caused Hmong leaders to withdraw their interest. "The racism was right below the surface," says Sister Clara. She promptly started an antiracism task force and held a three-day seminar to educate and sensitize the townspeople. The message is now being taken into the area schools.

Yet, the people in these five parishes—with the assistance of five quite diverse individuals—struggle to be a people of God, something perhaps best seen during a visit to one of their small Christian communities.

At the neat home of Austin and Irene McGeary (Kevin's parents) on Marysland Street in Danvers, seven members of the Church of the Visitation confront the three questions of the week. As with much of life, there are no apocalyptic moments of blinding saintliness, rather the ordinariness of struggling to be just and decent, to find inspiration and guidance in the muddle of daily life. The question about "a person who was strong in conviction but gentle in approach" seems to resonate. No one wanted to be "gobbled up" by someone else's agenda, one woman admits. Rather, they look for gentle persuasion, so that they might decide the best path on their own. Yes, this reflected the life of Jesus and, closer to home, they found this quality in their own Sister Clara. It was a quality they all vowed to try to practice play that week.

Weariness, the topic of the third question, sets in when you have tried to do everything yourself instead of...well, instead of depending on the strength of God. A visitor can almost see that yoke of Christian belief and practice hoisted onto seven sets of shoulders—and being found amazingly light.

And they wanted to lift one another's burdens. That lady in church whom everyone knows is going through a rough time and has gained more weight than she cares to acknowledge? One member of the group saw her come in for Mass last Sunday with the longest, saddest look on her face, but wearing a bright polka-dot dress. She bypassed the face and complimented the dress. The woman beamed.

When we adjourn for brats and beer at the Danvers Liquor Store—which is a restaurant, meeting place and bar—it seems that almost everyone in the whole town is there, all ninety-six of them. Conversation passes easily over the Formica tables, and one can clearly see how important the church just up Washington Avenue is to them. Church gatherings are the main social events; the priests and nuns, their common bond; religious belief is a common currency and a continuing challenge.

As I drive out of town and into the open country-side where clear, open fields belie the fact that houses once dotted the landscape—and that some family farms have disappeared without a trace—I am reas-sured to know that the Church has not left these brave and good people. They are the unknown and unsung heroes and heroines who not only feed us, but a good portion of the world. While farming is done on a larger and larger scale, they have kept the intimacy of rural life alive. Independent and rugged as farmers have always been, they have proved themselves people who can also do things together. Small things, impor-tant things, holy things.

Holy Family

2515 Palatine Road
Inverness, Illinois 60067
(847) 359-0042
www.holyfamilyparish.org

✦   POINTS OF EXCELLENCE: ✦

1. Family-Conscious Ministry

2. Communications Ministry: Beyond the Walls

3. Relevant Homilies—Linking Life to Faith to Life

As people flocked to the Willowcreek Community Church in the gently rolling hills in what was then primarily farmland northwest of Chicago, the Catholic Church took notice, for good reason. Not only was Willowcreek a new kind of a religious institution, affiliated with none of the mainline denominations, but ex-Catholics made up 60 to 75 percent of its membership. Something desperately wrong had happened during Catholicism's move from the tightly knit, often ethnic neighborhoods in the heart of Chicago to the suburbs. Too many in the suburban Diaspora believed that the Church of their childhood had not met or even acknowledged their needs as adults.

In the archdiocesan offices of Joseph Cardinal Bernardin, the decision was made in 1984 to take a hard look at—if not exactly replicate—Willowcreek's obvious appeal. First, the diocese held a series of meetings in Catholic homes, then services in a local public high school cafeteria and finally, after a three-year and sometimes painful discernment process, purchased sixteen acres of farmland and founded a new parish community, Holy Family.

Today, the sprawl of middle- and upper-middle-class homes has completely enveloped the Holy Family

Father Patrick Brennan and visiting priest,
Father William Kenneally

grounds. There, flanked by a sprawling parking lot that speaks to the crowds that flock from neighboring towns, sits an impressive glass and stone structure. Vaguely monastic in its soaring simplicity, the Holy Family buildings comprise a virtually self-contained small community: an 1,800-seat church, a maze of offices to support its 120 ministries and 28-person staff, meeting spaces and classrooms, a nursery, kitchen, chapel, even a rectory. A 5.5-million-dollar construction project has added that classic Catholic structure—a gymnasium—as well as more office and activity space.

Joe Scaletta, like many at Holy Family, had been "lost and searching." This fifty-one-year-old electrical engineer seriously considered leaving the Catholic faith that had been in his family for generations. He—and many others—found Willowcreek extremely appealing. The local Catholic churches paled by comparison, and area Catholics were fed up with uninspiring priests and "tired" parishes. As Dave Rosanova puts it: "If we hadn't found Holy Family, we might not be in the Church today." He is not alone. During my visit to Holy Family, dozens of other parishioners say the same thing.

Today Holy Family is a huge parish with over three-thousand families, some ten-thousand people in all. Yet the *Official Catholic Directory*, which lists all parishes and priests, lists only one priest in residence. While this certainly testifies to the shortage of priests these days, for such a parish would have had three or four priests a generation ago, the *Directory* can quantify neither the depth and breadth of lay involvement in the actual ministries of this church nor the real transference of not only rights but responsibility from clergy to laity.

Some may consider Holy Family a model of collaboration—that oft-used and misused buzzword in today's priest-poor American Catholic Church. The word *collaboration* must be used with great caution these days. That hit home a few years ago as I looked into the unblinking eyes of two firm-jawed young men preparing for ordination at one of America's most renowned seminaries. I understood clearly what they meant by the term. *Collaboration* meant that the pastor would tell laypeople what to do, just as he had once told his curates, and they would do it.

Collaboration, in fact, is not a word often used at Holy Family. Instead, its pastor, fifty-two-year-old Father Patrick Brennan, uses the term *lateral ministries.* This signals that the playing field is level and that anyone expecting or wanting him to carry the ball all the time will be disappointed.

No one complains about the shortage of priests at Holy Family. In fact, Father Brennan has repeatedly said he would sooner have a committed, competent, faith-filled lay person than simply another Roman collar around the neck of a fellow priest who did not share the vision and was reluctant to do the work of a church like Holy Family.

Father Brennan's path to Holy Family is an interesting pilgrimage in itself, fraught with not a few disappointments. When the diocese proposed the new church, he applied for the pastor's position but was passed over in favor of Father Medard Laz, who had greater financial expertise. When Father Laz, exhausted by 100-hour weeks, wanted to move on in 1993, Father Brennan, along with twelve others, applied for the job. Once apprised of the breadth and complexity of Holy Family's ministries and of the intensity and expectations of lay staff and volunteers (and their willingness to stand up to the pastor), ten dropped out. The eleventh eventually did too, leaving the lone remaining candidate, Father Brennan, to head what is considered one of the jewels in the crown of the Archdiocese of Chicago.

It was a perfect match for this spiritual, yet self-described "dark-souled Irishman." Brennan had attended a Tom Peters' "In Search of Excellence" seminar and had learned about a new model for parish structure, attitude and approach. When he had served as head of the archdiocesan evangelization office, he had advised other pastors on what to do. Now in a parish, he felt eager to put the ideas into practice.

"It was clear to me that a parish had to focus on three things if it was to meet the needs of, for lack of a better word, the 'new' Catholic," he says as we talk in the rectory late one night. The rectory itself symbolizes the organic quality of Holy Family; its entrance is off a corridor of the office complex, providing a private space for the priest yet keeping him accessible to his parishioners. Father Brennan, a slightly built man with thinning, curly auburn hair, speaks in a voice at once modest in modulation and firm in conviction. He is not the powerhouse personality one might expect to find leading such a large and successful parish. In fact, he has a certain boyish shyness about him.

"First, we had to offer a family-conscious ministry that continually involved all members of the family, not just the kids as they prepared for first communion

---

✦ 1. FAMILY-CONSCIOUS MINISTRY ✦

"Parishes can be too involved with the individual—just like the culture—and fail to see all the relationships that really matter," says Father Patrick Brennan. At Holy Family, children's religious education has moved away from focusing on only the children and instead includes the entire family—whoever makes up that family. Common Sense Parenting, a program brought in from Boys Town, and marriage enrichment classes teach Catholic values and practice to the entire family unit and not just to certain members, isolated by age. "We teach that the basic cell of the reign of God is the home, the family, and it is here that Catholicism is first lived out, not in church. And when you bring all the members together so they can hear the same message, it becomes common currency in the home."

or later, for marriage," he continues. "Second, small communities are absolutely crucial so that people are involved in faith-sharing spirituality rather than the kind of mindless voluntecrism that marks too much of what we think of as 'successful' churches. And third, adult education. We had to address the fact that many Catholics stopped learning and being taught when they walked out of Catholic school or their last CCD class.

"And we had to do all this primarily with laypeople. All those brothers and sisters and priests that we depended upon for decades were gone and they weren't coming back."

After a few years at Holy Family, Father Brennan added two more crucial elements, one old-fashioned and the other new. "I quickly saw, now that I was a pastor at ground zero myself and not just advising pastors what to do, that we had to *do* much better at basic pastoral work. Our funerals had to reach and touch the bereaved and their friends. We had to find new ways of counseling so that modern men and women, more used to going to their therapist than to a church, might see that spirituality and mental health really go hand-in-hand.

"And we had to communicate better. Sunday-morning notices just weren't enough." Today, in addition to Father Brennan's radio and cable television shows, Holy Family bulletins are sent to each home monthly, small faith communities receive specific guidelines for their weekly meetings, homilies are

✦ 2. COMMUNICATIONS MINISTRY: BEYOND THE WALLS ✦

The slick, Hollywood-style presentations of televangelists have probably discouraged many Catholic parishes from forming any sort of communications ministry, but "unless you have one," says Father Patrick Brennan, "you're preaching to the choir, not the unchurched, who probably need what happens in the parish as much or more than the people in the pews." While Holy Family's size and resources allow for a full communications ministry, Father Brennan believes that "every parish can do something. I saw an ad for a local pizza joint on one of the major cable networks and found that local-access spots are actually pretty cheap, so we put together some talking heads addressing meaning, healing, belonging and family, and basically said, 'If you're looking for this in your life, come to us.' I'm talking Nickelodeon, A&E, TNT, CNN—places where people might not expect such an invitation. Our Web site—and every parish has someone who can design one, even kids can do it—brings in people all the time. We have Mass on the radio and through a local cable franchise. We tuck our bulletin into the local suburban paper that is sent to all forty-thousand people who live right around us."

offered on tape for the homebound and an attractive
Internet site provides a gateway to the church's many
opportunities and ministries. Newspaper ads high-
lighting specific programs bring in new people each
week.

A few recent weekday nights at Holy Family under-
score the range of ministries (they are decidedly not
called programs or activities) at Holy Family. The
Phoenix support group for the separated and divorced
hosted a speaker who discussed enhancing dating and
relationship skills, and the Be Joyful Again gathering
talked of the pain experienced upon the deaths of their
spouses and their efforts to find wholeness again. The
Respect Life group prayed the rosary in the sanctuary,
a men's ministry prayer group gathered in the chapel
and a mediation group met in a nearby house. Spiritual
partnering, Knights of Columbus, support for victims
of domestic violence and a unique group called
WESOM (We Saved Our Marriage), which deals with
how to heal after an adulterous affair, contribute to the
Holy Family mix.

In one of the original farm buildings beyond the
parking lot is a counseling clinic, open from 9 A.M.
to 9 P.M. A brilliant meeting of need and available
resources provides therapists-in-training (Father
Brennan himself is completing studies for a Ph.D. in
psychology) at a fraction of cost.

"I think *need* is a key word we in church ministry
have to constantly address," Father Brennan says. "We
are a church that seeks to discover people's needs they

don't even know that they have. And then to meet them in a place that is undergirded by a rich religious tradition and staffed with those not necessarily with religious degrees, but with the appropriate talents."

Sue Werner speaks for many seekers: "My prayer life was just as it had been when I was a child and self-help books were becoming tiresome and priests I had approached were uninterested and unable to help." At Holy Family, the needs of Sue and other parishioners were acknowledged and met. There they encountered a deeper spirituality and, even more importantly to many, found that Father Brennan treated them as adults. His sermons linked the "News of the Week" with the "Good News." A "high intellectual level" is how one parishioner describes it. "Father Brennan holds the newspaper in one hand and the Bible in the other," says another. In addition to the great homilies, superb adult education features both Father Brennan's insights and those of outside speakers.

Yet, this still-young parish clearly envisions membership as a two-way street. "The atmosphere at Holy Family creates a culture of involvement," says Janet Hauter, a fifty-two-year-old management consultant. "So many people say after attending Holy Family a couple of times, 'I found a home.'" And having found that home, parishioners willingly jump into activities. This is not mindless volunteerism, but meaningful service. The parish even offers programs in discernment "to help you discover for yourself where your gifts are best used to do God's work," says Mary Whitside, a thirty-

five-year-old homemaker. Mary, whose Southern
Baptist husband eventually went through RCIA, helps
to lead the Christian Family Movement in the parish.

Scores of both Catholic and Protestant churches
have many and varied programs, although perhaps not
the profusion found at Holy Family. To me, what
makes Holy Family different is that, while still in many
respects a traditional Catholic parish, it is mission driven and lay driven. It isn't dogma driven or hierarchical. Father Brennan looks upon the eight laypeople
who head the major ministering communities (worship, family life, communications, outreach and social
justice, evangelization and catechesis, pastoral care,
operations, youth) as associate pastors. "I try to bring
order out of chaos," Father Brennan says with a wry
smile on his face. "I am at once in charge and not in
charge at all."

From making meals for new mothers to protesting
the School of the Americas, from Kathy Ross standing
up to the local police who wanted to evict some
homeless people from makeshift shelters and drive
them out of town to Jean Glover's work with a
divorced and widowed group, Holy Family parishioners are a powerful presence in this part of suburban
Chicago. The church tithes 10 percent of its budget to
social outreach causes, the homeless, elderly, kids aca-
demically at risk and the mentally retarded.

And if one tried to locate the soul of Holy Family,
one might point to the enormous acrylic crucifix that
looms over the altar. Conceived and constructed at a

Continuous education

staggering cost of $800,000, this work of art has a high emotional as well as actual price tag. The Cross of New Life, as it is called, depicts Christ bursting out of the cross, his hair streaming back from his fine-featured face, his hand thrust out to the people in the pews. The cross cannot contain his power; in fact it serves as his launching pad, the source of his might. The message is clear: Suffering, betrayal, disappointment and even death need not stop or inhibit you. Reach up and take this hand. Then go out into the world. His force is with you, each one of you.

"When I walked into the church and saw the Cross of New Life, it made me feel as if I had arrived home after a long journey," says Dawn Watkiss. "I was drawn into it," adds Susette Leonard, who had been away from the Church for twenty years. "I had a sense of God's presence." This presence and this parish have sustained Susette through a difficult divorce.

Dioceses across America have launched program upon program for the purpose of evangelization. At Holy Family it takes place quite naturally: by word of mouth. When Barb Knuth, who runs a construction company, talks about Father Brennan's sermons at lunch, she is not just trolling for converts. She has found something wonderful for her life and wants other people to know.

"I feel a surge of faith at this place," says another parishioner. "I used to fulfill my 'duty,' now I can't wait to get here." Joy Micheletto, a preschool teacher, admits being a Catholic of the "old-school teachings" who has found a new faith at Holy Family. "To be part of a caring community, to have a church that helps with my spiritual development—I tell people all the time about our church."

Joanne Dunham, a young mother, calls it an "evangelical Catholic church." High praise, indeed, this hybrid term.

Although certainly an exemplary parish, Holy Family has its tensions and its problem areas. It is an unremittingly white congregation and decidedly middle class at a minimum. Some members, especially those hurt by the Church's restrictive practices or its treatment during a divorce, abortion or otherwise difficult time in their lives, feel freed at Holy Family. They are charting a new path and recoil at Father Brennan's insistence on church rubrics, saying, "That's a bit too Catholic, isn't it, Pat?"

Yet Father Brennan doesn't relent. "He keeps on

saying he is calling us to a radical union with one another," one parishioner whispers to me, as if the subject were too hot to confront directly. "Hey, that's tough. I don't like to hear it all the time. I don't like everybody in this church. But this is my family. Am I just going to walk away because we have a fight or a disagreement or two?"

When I visited Holy Family near Valentine's Day on World Recommitment Sunday, couples were asked to stand up and renew their marriage vows. Two men

✦ 3. RELEVANT HOMILIES — LINKING LIFE TO FAITH TO LIFE ✦

In Father Patrick Brennan's experience, the best homilies write themselves. "But our problem as priests is that we want to show how much we know rather than how human we are."

For Father Brennan, the process of writing his homily begins on Monday morning, when he reads the scripture for that weekend's liturgies. "Then I start listening." The phrase "breaking open the Word" is often used in Catholic circles, but not always used well. Father Brennan has that week's scripture read in staff meetings and in small groups; it is on his mind as he reads the newspapers or a book, as he drives in his car, eats his meals. He also quietly rose to their feet, hands entwined. This did not go down easily in suburban Inverness. After a collective gulp from those who saw or heard about this couple, parish life went on.

One Sunday morning, having preached about bringing a generous spirit into the week, Father Brennan pauses at the end of Mass and says, "Think of one way you'll be more hospitable, kinder to someone you have difficulty with. Stand up and leave when you're ready." In silence, the parishioners ponder his words

consults standard sources, such as commentaries, so that his homily has a sound basis, "but   and this might sound narcissistic—I keep asking, 'What is this passage saying to me?' I'm a pretty ordinary guy and if I can answer that question I know I'll be speaking to the experience of a lot of people out there. Anxiety, despair, anger, difficult relationships—aren't we all going through these things? This is a psychological generation, so there is nothing wrong in addressing those issues, meanwhile being not just a motivational speaker, but a conduit of revelation. The eventual sermon is a redaction of the week's events and insights. When I try to make it a theological sermon, heavy on Christology and institutional issues, I inevitably fail. When I stick close to my own experience, it is always, always more successful. Not breast beating, just an honest appraisal of where I am on my own spiritual journey."

and his challenge. One by one, they quietly walk from the church.

There is an ever present tension between the demands of Catholic orthodoxy and the promise of Vatican II vision. Holy Family could easily become another popular, feel-good place that reduces religion to social work and Catholicism to hollow ritual or a church where rebellious parishioners proudly flaunt episcopal oversight at any opportunity. Being a cutting-edge parish means being careful with such an impressive tool; it can slice through your flesh as well as cut through disaffection and religious ennui. Yet something has happened here: The new has indeed been recreated from the ancient wisdom of the scripture, the promise of forgiveness, the embrace of community.

As I sit alone before the Cross of New Life late one evening, the cross confronts me with the reality that, like Christ, all of us are crucified in our lives—by disease or misfortune or deceit or even our innate limitations—and yet there is a far greater power if we only would summon it.

In the silence of an empty church, with a single light on that cross, I have the sense that the power which that ton of clear plastic represents is being continually and unequivocally offered to the people of Holy Family. For their part, they need but to extend their hands—in boldness or timidity, strength or weakness, whatever they might have to offer. God's hand has already reached out to them.

St. Peter Claver

1923 St. Philip Street
New Orleans, Louisiana 70116-2199
(504) 822-8059

✦ POINTS OF EXCELLENCE: ✦

1. Pastor as Missionary

2. Church-Based Community Organizing

3. Liturgy as Canvas to Be Embellished Upon

When the visiting prelate's very efficient master of ceremonies called to arrange a visit to St. Peter Claver Church, he detailed exactly what the visit should entail, listing the customary components for such an event and the prelate's desires. Father Michael

Jacques, the pastor of St. Peter's, listened patiently, awaiting the end of the list.

When he had finished, Father Jacques replied that the people of St. Peter's would be honored by such a visit, and they would welcome the prelate into their midst. But, he continued, they would not want to approach it that way.

On the appointed Sunday, in fact, the parish would go on exactly as if the prelate were not there at all. Merely conforming to a stylized agenda would be out of character at St. Peter's. They would warmly welcome the prelate but would offer none of the ecclesial obeisance typical of such affairs. And, as Father Jacques obliquely pointed out, there was actually no need to do something special for the event. While being thoroughly Catholic, this church did not routinely go through the motions on any occasion; neither did it feel hemmed in by custom. Being extraordinary was quite ordinary at St. Peter's.

The prelate came one Sunday morning and, with fierce drumming and elegant dancing, the parishioners welcomed him as the chieftain he was. By the end of the liturgy, tears streamed down his face. He had never in all his parish visits, he admitted, choked with emotion, had such an experience.

If this little moment in the life of St. Peter Claver dramatizes anything, it is the fact that this parish combines a spirit of generosity and of welcoming with a feisty confidence rarely found in the Catholic-parish world. Realizing where all this is happening underscores the miracle of this New Orleans parish.

On my initial visit to St. Peter's, the cab driver peered warily into his rear view mirror when I give him the address: 1923 St. Philip Street. Then he turns to face me and asks, "Are you sure about that?" Those are his words, but his unspoken question is clearly, "Are you nuts or something, going into that neighborhood?" 1923 St. Philip Street *is* in Treme, an area with the reputation of being one of New Orleans' worst. It is riddled by drugs, prostitution, poverty, abandoned houses and buildings; to many it represents the stereotype of urban blight.

The Treme area of New Orleans, with its narrow, "shotgun" houses—so called because a shell could be fired through the front door and emerge from the back without ever hitting a wall   had always been considered a working-class, reasonably integrated neighborhood. In a strange twist of fate, the Civil Rights Act, which formally legislated integration, accomplished just the opposite. After white flight, Treme became a totally black neighborhood, home to the working poor who could not escape to outlying areas.

Despite the razor wire atop the chain-link fences around its playgrounds and open areas, the whitewashed stucco church at 1923 *is* a beacon to the predominantly African American community, an amazing place not only of hope, but also of solid accomplishment and power. This Catholic church has proved a force to be reckoned with, both in the neighborhood and in the city at large.

St. Peter Claver had created a proud tradition since its founding in 1920; the grade school had educated a good number of black leaders and professional people. However, by the mid-1980s it had only six hundred families on its rolls, the collection totaled a dismal thousand dollars a week, and few attended Mass there, fearing to enter what was then New Orleans' highest crime area. Rumors that it would soon be closed abounded.

In 1984 the Society of St. Edmund, a small religious order now numbering only eighty-five in America, appointed a most unlikely pastor. Father Jacques, a native of Maine, was white. He had started in religious life as an Edmundite brother, serving for a time as a cook. His had all the earmarks of an inauspicious religious career, and his ordination to the priesthood was almost a fluke. When Father Jacques arrived at St. Peter's and looked around his new, rundown assignment, he saw not devastation but potential, not black Catholics who needed to be more Catholic but, rather, needed to be more black—*and* Catholic. He approached his new assignment almost as if he had been sent to a foreign country. He needed to understand the culture of the people of St. Peter Claver, the people on the dismal blocks surrounding the parish, the people who had once proudly attended but who now rarely returned to their old neighborhood. As in an earlier era, he went door to door talking to the people. They told him of the problems: Absentee landlords ran buildings into the ground, then abandoned them; the parish school was terrible; streets were unsafe; drug traffic proliferated. Hope was considered a foolish concept.

✦ 1. Pastor as Missionary ✦

"I think what might be beneficial for any person coming into a parish—regardless of where it is—is to try to suspend your preconceptions, what you think the place and the people are about and just go into it as if it were a foreign land, completely alien to you," says Father Michael Jacques. "I was fortunate to have Xavier University to teach me about the Afrocentric world, but I think that too often we priests go in with our own agenda of what needs to be done, the idea that we are going to teach. Instead, we have to be ready to *learn*, to understand what it is that is important to our people. And you have to be willing to be rejected, to be considered a naïve fool. But when people know you are really interested in who they are, they will open up to you. We have 2,600 families, and I and some 50 trained volunteers went door to door and visited at least half of them just to find out what was on their minds. We weren't talking about parish membership or church attendance. That would come in time. And what they wanted was empowerment, so they could speak for themselves, ownership; and they wanted to be versed in their own culture, not the white American culture. Don't say much and the people will let you know their needs. Then set about to meet them."

After familiarizing himself with the area and its residents, Father Jacques traveled to Xavier, New Orleans' premier black university, to educate himself about a people and a culture mainstream Catholicism knew very little about. "I had Avery Dulles's five models of the church—herald, sacrament, institution, servant, community—in mind, but to make that happen at St. Peter's, I needed to be schooled in a whole new theology, not Eurocentric but Afrocentric," Father Jacques recalls. Among his teachers was the legendary black nun, Sister Thea Bowman. Slowly, he began to put into practice what he learned.

Despite his efforts, parishioners regarded him somewhat warily during the first two years; he did not receive a single invitation to a wedding or baptism reception. He appalled older members of the church by incorporating modest dollops of African music and dance into the liturgy. For them, adaptation to the white world was the key to success.

"You have to realize how unique this was for our community," says Alena Boucree, thirty-eight. "Our culture had never been integrated into the church. It was absolutely separate, as if it was so inferior that it shouldn't be allowed to taint this pristine, uniform Catholic image. Father Michael was showing us something about ourselves we didn't quite realize was there. After all, the Saints Perpetua and Felicity, whom we pray to in every Mass, are not only women; they are black women. Most of us didn't know that."

St. Peter Claver choir

"Most Catholics don't realize how beautifully, naturally, the Afrocentric world and values fit with Catholicism," says Father Jacques as we walk down the main aisle of his church, quiet now on a Friday afternoon. An impressive place, it has a high, vaulted Gothic ceiling interlaced with wood molding. My eye stops at a brilliant green backdrop to the altar, accentuated by intricately patterned yellow and green kente cloth. The Coptic cross on the altar is surrounded by two circles, the larger, outside circle symbolizing God eternal and the inside cross touching all creation, the four corners of the earth.

Father Jacques, fifty, wearing a green dashiki to coordinate with the color of the liturgical season, hardly looks like a fiery-eyed revolutionary. He has a kindly, open face, a grey-flecked beard and could easily passed unnoticed on a street. He sometimes appears a bit distracted, but when he focuses in on a person or an issue—or talks about the magnificence of his parishioners—his eyes show laser-beam intensity.

"These principles," he says, pointing to the banners hanging above, "are these not exactly what Christianity is about?" He reads off the principles and explains their meaning:

> *Umoja*—unity; we are in this together.
> *Kujichagulia*—self-determination; speaking for ourselves.
> *Ujima*—responsibility; working together.
> *Ujamaa*—cooperation; building community.
> *Nia*—purpose; working together toward a goal.
> *Kuumba*—creativity; sharing our talents.
> *Imani*—faith; being believers in Jesus Christ, parents, teachers, our leaders.

"As I got further and further into studying African culture and values, I slowly realized the synergism. Is it *ujima*, working together, or Galatians 5:14, 'Out of love, place yourself at each other's service'? Is it *kuumba*, creativity, or 1 Corinthians 4, 'There are different gifts, but the same spirit'? This is a match of cultures made in heaven. Meanwhile, as I was learning—and they were learning with me—a lot was happening in New Orleans, which is a predominantly Catholic city. The Full Gospel movement was having an enormous, visceral appeal for Catholics because they weren't finding that kind of vitality in their own parishes. We just couldn't do the Mass the same way we'd been doing it for years because if we did, we would have little appeal, especially to younger African Americans, and the church would close. We had to blend what was best and most natural in the African culture with what was best—when you stripped away all the Eurocentric overlays that we have come to assume are the essence of Catholicism—in our faith. To be honest, it was easy once they were liberated from self-doubt and self-hate and allowed to see their unique spirituality."

As I talk to St. Peter Claver parishioners in the newly refurbished kitchen of the rectory (which is filled with African art, batiks and masks) or on the curbside in front of a church that has turned New Orleans' highest crime area into one of the *lowest* in the city, I hear numerous testaments to the work of this priest and his people.

"I was born a Baptist," says Derek Wells, thirty-three, "and believe me, I didn't join *the* Catholic Church; I joined *this* Catholic church. There was something magical about it, the good feeling you had just being here, the feeling that 'I can do this.' And what I've seen happen in the lives of the kids, especially young black males. This return to African tradition captures their imagination. When they hear a drumbeat, they feel something deep within them.

They want more and more of their culture and its values because it is theirs and it is good. They begin to know who they are. This is true identity."

Don Boucree, Alena's husband, recalls a popular story. All black families in a neighborhood—except for one family—switched over from a white iceman to a black iceman when he offered his services. "Why did one family stay with the white iceman? 'Because white ice is colder,' we said. 'No,' Father Michael said to us, 'your ice is just as cold.' He gave us our heritage back, connected us with our past so we knew who we were. And only when you know who you are can you take responsibility for your life. All through those years Father was being educated and so were we. He has a remarkable openness to change. And he's good at affirmation: He tells us, 'You are great. You have unique talents.' We began believing in ourselves."

By any measure, St. Peter Claver is an impressive parish. It has a top-notch grade school, which not only offers an extended school day, but also after-school and Saturday activities to keep the children off what are safer, but still mean streets. Fully 70 percent of its students actually belong to the parish, a staggeringly high number in New Orleans, where many consider parish schools the best alternative to a weak public school system and tuition payments rather than parish membership drive the enrollment. In addition, St. Peter has a small satellite school for sixty boys in the fifth through the eighth grades who have had difficulties at home or in the courts, where Father Jacques will intercede so young people end up in his school and not in jail. The school is run entirely by volunteer teachers, mostly young college graduates. School children visit the holy places of the Civil Rights movement—Tuskegee, Montgomery, Selma—so they might encounter their more recent history.

The parish also founded Claver Federal Credit Union so local people could eventually buy their homes, which absentee landlords often own. Lay leadership is at an astounding level; 115 parishioners recently completed a lay training course. And while Father Jacques relies on legions of volunteers, he hires excellent staff members. An eight-person staff covers religious education, social ministries, youth, music, bereavement and liturgical dance, which is a priority in this parish. Although 80 percent of its parishioners have incomes below the poverty level, its collection level ranks tenth among New Orleans' 156 parishes. The parish collects over $18,000 on an average Sunday; many people tithe, and the membership has surged to 2,500 families.

One afternoon, Father Jacques and I sit in his comfortable living room on the second floor of the rectory and talk about this parish and about African American Catholics, which number some two-million.

"We found that the standard 'white' Eucharist and hymns and general way of doing things really don't work well for African Americans," he begins. "When I traveled to Africa and saw how dancing is a natural part of life, how elders are regarded, how joyously

Liturgical dance

they celebrate, I realized what we had to do. For these are a royal people. Europeans came to America with an identity. Africans were stripped of their identity and it has to be returned to them. But this doesn't mean you take one or the other. You can be thoroughly African American while being thoroughly Catholic. We say the rosary here; we do litanies; we venerate saints, the blessed sacrament.

"If any people should be angry, not only at America, but at the Catholic Church, it is African Americans. But they are not. They identify with the oppression of the Israelites, but they also know about the liberation God can provide. The African tree of life has people standing on each other's shoulders. This is a deep and authentic spirituality that should be spread. These people are alive in the spirit. And you know what?" (His eyes, focused as laser beams, fix on me.) "It is the black Church that is going to revolutionize the white Church in this country. If . . . if we only have the good sense to allow it to happen."

What I continually find striking about St. Peter's is that it possesses a combination of generosity and steely determination, somewhat like its pastor. Generosity might seem an unlikely quality in a poor neighborhood and on the streets of "the Big Easy," a city with a nationally known high crime rate. However, St. Peter Claver, reflecting traits within the African American world itself, continually lives out its Catholicity in small, but surprising ways. When a benefit dinner held at the church had a good amount of food left over, the organizers sent it to a local homeless shelter. They did so despite the fact that many of them lived in poverty and perhaps wondered where they would find the next day's meals. A school full of children, many of whom also live below the poverty level, collected $5,000 to help a school in Nairobi. "That's the beauty of these people," says Father Jacques. "They have experienced pain, rejection and hate, and yet they come back with love and the attitude that there is always someone else who needs help more than they do. Reconciliation comes naturally for them. Their faith continually energizes me."

As for the grit, determination and ability to organize of St. Peter's people, one finds no greater proof than the crime statistics of the First District. This has become a safer neighborhood in large part because of

✦ 2. CHURCH-BASED COMMUNITY ORGANIZING ✦

"The Church stands for human rights, so why shouldn't the parish be the center for not only human, but civil rights?" asks Father Michael Jacques. "The whole Civil Rights movement was church-based; why shouldn't that continue? Are the problems solved?" As he looked out over his poor and dangerous neighborhood, he knew he could not tackle its problems alone or without expert help. He and parish members attended workshops in church-based community organizing, then had expert organizers come to New Orleans to survey the problems and advise them. Simultaneously, using the "one-to-one" approach, he and volunteers visited homes and discerned what the neighborhood saw as its major problems: drug activity, crime, prostitution, abandoned houses. "As the Book of Proverbs tells us, 'A people without a vision will perish,'" says Father Jacques. "Now we had the vision. We started small, but then it built up. We put our block watches into effect, built up a good relationship with the local precinct and just kept on going. We marched through the neighborhood; we marched on city hall. The people were fired up with the vision that they had the power to make things change."

the "hot spot" sheets that parishioners hand in to the pastor, who then forwards them to the local police station. Father Jacques, in essence, helped organize a massive, church-based community watch system. Parishioners put an end to the conspiracy of silence that pervades poor neighborhoods, in which people long accustomed to police neglect and sometimes even brutality not only feel hopeless to fight criminals but also have concerns about possible retribution. "When it not only becomes acceptable, but a faith imperative to report drug trafficking or prostitution, then something begins to happen," says Father Jacques. "The community takes on a new pride. They aren't going to put up with it anymore. This is evangelizing in the best sense, making Christ present in the community. When ownership and responsibility are infused with religious values, it is unbeatable."

After years of these "hot spot" reports—and Father Jacques's persistent follow-up—the precinct captain and city officials now call St. Peter's before they do anything in the neighborhood. The fact that a thousand people or so just might show up for a demonstration causes them to take St. Peter Claver and Father Michael Jacques very seriously.

On a recent Sunday, both the mayor and the district attorney attended a morning liturgy during which the congregation, en masse, marched out to the site of an abandoned building to dramatize their demand that the city act to bring absentee landlords to court. That television crews covered the event was not an accident. Father Jacques is hardly shy about assuring the right kind of publicity for his causes.

In a strange turn of events, St. Ann's, which split off from St. Peter's decades ago to build a church exclusively for whites a few blocks away, closed some years past. Its abandoned buildings had been a neighborhood eyesore, but now St. Peter's plans to convert them into senior citizens' housing and a seniors' dining hall.

Father Jacques is a driven, focused man. One parishioner lovingly categorized him as a "control freak." But he doesn't rule free of the feedback and wisdom of his congregation. At such times, it is not uncommon for a comment to set him right. "Father, you're acting very 'white' right now," is just one of them.

St. Peter Claver is a powerful presence in its community, and the unifying force that focuses all that energy and then returns it to the streets is surely the Sunday liturgies. The liturgy at St. Peter's is unlike anything I—or the vast majority of American Catholics—have ever experienced before. The period since Vatican II has seen an array of liturgical innovations. Many have been quite positive, but others have a somewhat tinny, forced feel to them. I, for one, dislike having a certain kind of false exhilaration almost demanded of me, especially when it does not grow naturally out of what is actually happening. That is certainly not the case at St. Peter Claver.

The Sunday I attend, the parish is celebrating Women's Day. A drumbeat sounds at the front of the church, in the best African tradition, calling the village

✦ 3. LITURGY AS CANVAS TO BE EMBELLISHED UPON ✦

At St. Peter's, the standard, accepted Catholic liturgy provides a beginning, not an end. "The Roman liturgy is basic, even stark," say Father Michael Jacques. "Once you understand its basic structure, it allows for great flexibility. There are too many things you can do to make it more relevant, more beautiful; it is a shame to just go through the same motions every week. You can be 100 percent Catholic and yet mold the liturgy to fit the occasion, to fit the personality of your congregation. We took courses in liturgy and Afrocentric culture at Xavier University; we attended workshops. We didn't know much at the beginning, but we were willing, open to learning. We sought out the absolutely best musicians. And we began to use drums, then dance and upbeat singing, poetry, art. It can be many other things for different groups, but we need to continually try to make the liturgy alive. Each week there should be something a little different, something that says, 'Somebody was thinking about this Sunday and this life of mine.'"

people to gather. A group of liturgical dancers, in brilliant yellow robes and led by Judy Richard-Legier, a part-time staff member hired for exactly this ministry, move down the aisle and into the altar area. How better to welcome the Lord into our midst? How better to approach the harvest table, where we would all be fed and fed abundantly? It suddenly seemed exactly right. An interpretive dance solo by Anrea Thomas gives new meaning to the meditation: "My Soul Just Opened Up." Her expressive body opens up the words. Moses Hogan—the acclaimed music director who happens to be a Baptist and has conducted choirs all over the country, including the Mormon Tabernacle Choir—leads an eighty-woman choir. They stand in black dresses, each with a single, tasteful strand of pearls and a swatch of kente cloth over one shoulder. These are women not only admired for their singing, which is resolute, focused, joyous. They are a force to be reckoned with. I would have followed them anywhere.

A lay guest speaker, Mother Shine from Philadelphia, gives the reflection, based on the biblical story of the Samaritan woman at the well. Mother Shine invokes the women to "find the right man for your life. 'Come and see,' that woman said to her friends, 'see this man and he will transform your life.' Yes, he will transform your life." The women in the packed church nod assent, as do the men and even teenagers. It is a remarkably young gathering, with Generation X, thirty-somethings and young parents well represented.

Father Jacques, although in Catholic vestments (accented, as are all his chasubles, with kente cloth), could easily pass for an evangelical preacher. He is a natural at the Pentecostal art of "call and response." "Is God good, or what?" he calls out. "Is Jesus here this morning?" He uses two invocations I particularly like. Although I had not heard them before, they have since embedded themselves in my mind: "Our God is an on-time God." "Our God is a way-maker God."

Singing, dancing, preaching, invoking, all weave naturally in and out of an unmistakably Catholic eucharistic celebration. And the accent is on *celebration*. At the words, "Let us give God thanks and praise," that directly precede the consecration, the congregation loudly applauds God to make their point. During various prayers throughout the liturgy, people join hands and spill over into the aisles, lest they not be totally joined. As the last song is sung, the last dance danced, I look down at my watch. It seems as if I'd been there for fifteen minutes, but it has been over two hours.

As I stand in the bright sunshine in front of an address that struck fear in a cabdriver's heart, I understand that St. Peter's has advanced the next step in Catholic parish development. In pre–Vatican II days, we called them all Catholic parishes and applauded uniformity and propriety. After Vatican II, as they embraced the news that faith should be lived beyond Sunday morning, the best parishes earned the right to be called Catholic communities. St. Peter Claver goes beyond even that; one could call it a Catholic village. It is a total, organic, holy place, not just where people gather together, but where life can be lived from within.

St. Francis of Assisi

330 SE 11th Avenue
Portland, Oregon 97214
(503) 232-5880

✦ POINTS OF EXCELLENCE: ✦

1. Lay Pastor Advantages

2. Social Justice—Up Close and Personal

3. Lay-Driven Liturgies

Writing about a parish bounded on one side by a park containing the promising words of a saint and on the other by a street containing a row of somewhat forbidding factories presents a problem. Where does one begin? To call St. Francis of Assisi unique would be a virtually meaningless understatement. To call it a parish on the cutting edge would be more than geographically correct.

Consider that:

✦   St. Francis may be the only Catholic parish in America with a sheltered parking area for shopping carts. These, the mobile repositories of the treasured possessions—and sometimes survival supplies—of some of the church's visitors, receive as much respect as their homeless owners and even require proper licensing. If left for a while during an unexpected sojourn, the parish watches over the carts until their rightful owners return to claim them.

✦   The Sunday prayer of the faithful includes the petition: "We pray for Pope John Paul; our archbishop, John; and our pastor, Valerie." *Pastor Valerie!?* Valerie Chapman, a divorced mother of six, may have the title of administrator in the *Official Catholic Directory*, but to her parishioners, to the priests who come here to preside at the liturgies, and to the homeless men and women who come to the parish dining hall each day for dinner, she is most decidedly the person in charge.

✦   The church looks like both a Trappist abbey and a Northwest mountain lodge. Built in 1939 of Douglas fir, St. Francis resembles one of those woodsy, national-park lodges on the outside. Yet its stark, high-ceilinged interior, bathed in pale yellow light, is decidedly monastic. The shelter of the ample portico just outside the front doors provides a gathering place for the predominantly middle-class worshipers who come for Mass as well as a temporary home for some of the neighborhood men.

When I arrive on a typically overcast Oregon morning and ring the bell at the St. Francis rectory, Ann Bowling, the parish secretary, eyes me a bit suspiciously. There I stand, bag at my feet, expectant look on my face. In this busy parish, at this particular time of the morning I don't compute—mail has not yet come in, mealtime is a few hours away and the dining hall has already opened, should the wayfarer need to rest. After I explain the reason for my visit, she invites me in.

She had mistaken me for one of the homeless brethren and, while not treating me unkindly, quickly helps me to realize the necessity for enforcing some sense of order. Otherwise, the normal confusion surrounding these Catholic outposts in the cities would collapse into utter chaos, an ever present, looming possibility.

A short time later, Valerie Chapman arrives at the parish office, a huge, thirty-two-room former rectory. She is not exactly what you might expect a Catholic pastor to look like. (But then again, what should a woman pastor look like?) She is forty-nine-years-old, a throwback to the '60s with her long hair, graying at

✦ 1. LAY PASTOR ADVANTAGES ✦

"I'm not a separate kind of Catholic," says Valerie Chapman. "I don't have any more job security than any of the parishioners. I pay bills; I have family concerns. I think this causes everyone to take more seriously their own baptism and to be confronted with the questions: What is ministry anyhow and who is supposed to do what?" Too often Catholics tend to put themselves, Chapman contends, into a category other than all the "holy people"—namely, the clergy and professed religious. At St. Francis those lines continually blur and "no one knows when God is calling any of us. This equalizing effect frees people, gets them out of roles they assume they are supposed to play. The priesthood of all believers takes on new meaning when, week after week, they see me on the altar, in the office, in the dining hall."

the temples, pulled back. She wears a flowered jumper, white blouse, and sweater with sleeves pushed up. Her face, free of makeup, often breaks into a smile, a sort of feline grin actually, and her laugh resounds through what was once a decidedly male preserve. It still amazes her that she is running an American Catholic parish and she makes no secret that she gets an enormous kick out of it.

"I was made for this job. What better training for

running a poor, inner-city parish than being a single mother, raising six kids on a shoestring?" She good-naturedly shrugs off those who might question her qualifications. In addition to the survival skills she learned as a parent, Valerie received an excellent academic preparation, earning a master's degree in education, with an emphasis on religious studies, plus healthy doses of sociology, psychology and theater arts. She is but one of thousands of laypeople who have completed religious studies and who will be joined by the thirty-thousand now in training. Together, they will not only work in but also lead parishes as the number of Catholics grows and the number of male ordained clergy shrinks. This new battalion of lay leaders receives a balanced education, both in matters of the spirit and the world, for they will live and walk in both.

Valerie's service in this "pastoral capacity" evolved out of the confluence of two crucial factors: one is broad-based and the other, while now specific to Portland, is becoming widespread. In 1983, the Church promulgated the revised Code of Canon Law, which governs Catholic practice. The revised Code allowed women significant new roles in the Church. Although a dramatic new approach was on the books, many local dioceses had neither the interest nor the will to implement it. Some found it too radical or unnecessary. This opening for women, combined with a shortage of priests in the Northwest, forced Portland years ago to look for alternatives to an ordained priest in every parish.

People often use the term "priestless parish" to classify parishes like St. Francis. While colloquially accurate, the canonically correct, if dubious, phrase is "parish without a resident priest." The number of such parishes, in which laypeople and women religious, in essence, act as pastors has grown dramatically. While virtually unheard of until the late 1970s, parishes *without* a resident priest numbered 210 in 1990; today an estimated 17 percent of some eighteen thousand parishes have no priest in residence. Six of these are in Portland. St. Francis is somewhat typical of the parish that has *nonpriests*, to coin another term for this new kind of Catholic pastor, assigned. We will certainly see more such parishes in the future. With an aging physical plant and in a poor section of the city, St. Francis was hardly considered a plum assignment. A string of priests had spent short periods of time there, some of them dividing their time between the parish and other duties. Valerie had worked part-time at St. Francis in religious education. The priest assigned to the parish, realizing he was in the early stages of Alzheimer's disease, gave her more and more responsibilities until finally recommending she take over the parish.

At first, Valerie thought, "Fat chance, a divorced mother of six." But then it happened: The diocese appointed her to a three-year term, which just concluded, and has renewed her contract for three more years.

"The future of the church," is how Father Chuck Lienert, the pastor of record (called the moderator), describes this parish. "And what happens is that with a layperson in charge, you have much more lay involvement, so the result is actually a parish that is able to do far more, not less, because of not having a priest here." Father Lienert meets once a week for an hour with Valerie and every two months with the parish council. He often says weekend Mass, but otherwise the parish is basically in the hands of women, Valerie, Sister Phyllis Jaszkowiak, who oversees maintenance, and Julie Cusimano, the social ministry director.

While hardly a study in traditional roles or efficiency, St. Francis has cultivated an admirable reputation far beyond Portland for being a place where "the Word is lived out." St. Francis has proved a gateway back for hundreds of lapsed or alienated Catholics and is a pioneer in lay-driven liturgy. It provides the classic example of a parish that takes its social justice responsibilities seriously, integrating a sort of modified Catholic

Lunchtime at the dining hall

Worker style into a somewhat mainstream congregation. As Father Lienert has witnessed: "It is a parish that welcomes whomever comes. You can be in cast-off clothes or designer clothes; nobody much cares. People don't mouth social-justice talk, they live it."

At the center of that commitment to social justice stands St. Francis Dining Hall, where some three hundred homeless, indigents and migrants are fed each day. But this is hardly a faceless soup line that only meets physical needs. Julie Cusimano, an attractive, vivacious twenty-three-year-old, oversees a program that provides substance abuse, job, and psychological counseling by paid professionals. Even more importantly, the dining hall offers a safe haven to men and women whose lives are so mobile. There they can sit down, play cards, make phone calls, take a shower, and collect mail. It is their clubroom, a place where they are treated with dignity. Valerie has made it clear that police are not to violate this precious space unless they see an actual crime in progress.

Beyond all that the dining room provides, it serves as a daily reminder to the parish of the words from its mission statement: " . . .to serve the neighborhood in its many needs, physical, spiritual and human." By attempting to anneal two outwardly disparate congregations—people of the pew and people of the streets—they strive " . . .to reach out rather than build a safe place to be."

In order to sustain this commitment to the poor and to the revitalization of the neighborhood, St. Francis

✦ 2. Social Justice—Up Close and Personal ✦

There are many places of conversion in Catholic life, but Valerie Chapman points to the dining hall at St. Francis as having a life-changing effect on many a parishioner. "When you are up close, looking into the face of a poor person, it cannot help but challenge you to think about who you are and how you live," she says. "There was a time when our progressive liturgy was emphasized because it was so innovative and popular. We had to grapple with the question: Is that who we really were? We saw that without contact with the poor, we were turning into an elitist club. How we meet Christ in one another—beginning with the people who come to our dining hall—is really what is important. This faith community has grown to see that faith is more than an hour on Sunday morning. That dining hall is a holy place, and when one of the guests comes into RCIA and into the fuller life of the parish, it is cause for great celebration. We really see the fullness of the body of Christ, and without the dining hall we would not have that opportunity."

devotes enormous time and energy to its spiritual life. The liturgy is the product of lay initiative; prayers and original music are lay written. Flutes, guitars, tambourines and a piano combine with uncharacteristically hearty (for Catholics) singing. A mime might perform one Sunday to dramatize the story of Jesus and his disciples on the road to Emmaus or some vignette from the life of St. Francis; on another, there might be a liturgical dance (with candles held aloft), or a storyteller will take the parishioners through the Red Sea with Moses to vividly recall the Exodus story.

To sit with the people of St. Francis on Easter Sunday morning as the first rays of the sun suffuse the stained glass on the eastern side of the church is to know that resurrection is indeed at hand, that light will triumph over darkness, the poor will be fed, the bills paid, more volunteers will come forward.

The same feeling prevails on Father's day, when the homeless man with long, unkempt hair stands alone as other fathers are surrounded by their loved ones. Soon he of downcast eyes has his own spontaneous family about him, standing with him, honoring him on this day, a scene at once so poignant and painful. Or when Bob, who had spent many years living under a bridge, completed RCIA and became a Catholic. His rising up from the baptismal pool, beard streaming with holy water, was the epitome of new life. But the wonderful ceremony was not enough; he was still homeless. The parish had to go another step further. He is now both caretaker and sole resident of the rectory/office building.

Many consider the homilies alone worth the trip to St. Francis. People travel from throughout the greater

✦ 3. LAY-DRIVEN LITURGIES ✦

While good liturgy comprises a major draw at St. Francis, parishioners have learned that if they want it to continue, they have to do it themselves. "Basically, we trust people to try their ideas, and while some may not work out as well as we all hoped they would, we are constantly open to new ideas," says Valerie Chapman. A liturgy committee screens ideas, often developing them further. "We don't just go with anything that someone dreams up, but our attitude is always to listen, see if it is both liturgically possible and useful and to keep an open mind. We sometimes seem a little disorganized, but I've found that people do pick up the slack and they pick up the pieces once they know the liturgy is theirs—not mine alone."

Portland area and beyond to attend. While Valerie, as a layperson, is not formally allowed to preach homilies, her rich "reflections" carefully weave scriptural exegesis with the vicissitudes of ordinary life. One Sunday she used a page from family life to illustrate the futility of violence. Her daughter wanted to go snowboarding with a friend, a friend Valerie didn't approve of. She thought of breaking the snowboard. *That* would have stopped her . . . but would it have sent the right message? Bombing to bring peace?

While such "reflections" straddle the edge of liturgical practice, Valerie Chapman remains both a loyal daughter of the Church and a smart woman. "What sense would it make to simply defy rubric to make some point that would wreak havoc on this parish community and have me thrown out? Canon law is a guide, not a whip; laws are not laws for laws' sake, but for people's good. We must always be careful what we take our risks over."

If, for instance, a lesbian couple asked to be married in the church (a request many pastors have been confronted with), Valerie would have to say no "The Church moves slowly and for good reason. Jesus is about radical reconciliation, but how many foolish mistakes we would have made if we weren't held back from doing what seems right at the moment."

As with its thoughtful approach to liturgy, the parish has also made adult spirituality a crucial element of parish life. A contemplative prayer group gathers together weekly to simply sit in silence and pray for the needs of the Church. A scripture class, taught by a local scholar, emphasizes how to bring the Word into being in people's lives. During my visit at St. Francis, a women's spirituality group, instead of its usual weekly meeting to engage scripture, provides a bittersweet send-off for one of its members. Clair Goodall is moving to Arizona, so after a dinner at a nearby Thai restaurant, the women stop in the shadow of an industrial building to encircle her and sing a farewell. It is a tearful, lovely adieu, spontaneous, heartfelt and thoroughly spiritual from a group that has been meeting for over nine years, sharing one another's triumphs and pains and even the suicide of one of its members.

Despite the success of St. Francis, the issue of women pastors in the Catholic Church remains a thorny one. The Church teaching and requirements of an all-male ordained clergy rest on Christ's maleness and on centuries-long tradition. Valerie Chapman, of course, can do nothing about her sex. The arguments for celibate, unmarried (and male) ordinands, which revolve around clergy being available to all people in a distributive way as the most efficacious model of service to others, falter a bit in the experience of this woman.

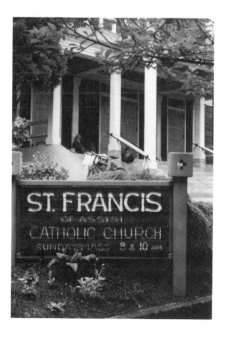

The sheltering portico

"Women approach things differently, mothers approach things even more differently," she says. "I listen. I don't always have the answers and so I think it's easier for people to fumble around for a solution with a woman. Somehow the 'father knows best' approach isn't always the best, and true consensus works better in the long run."

In her book, *They Call Her Pastor*, Ruth Wallace writes of the advantages of women leading a parish. Something as simple as women having a higher "approachability factor" caused people to more readily come to a woman pastor with their problems and concerns. Women were found to have more personal warmth and openness as well as what Wallace calls a "heart of compassion" in dealing both with parishes and parishioners. Women were better at building community.

While this parish and its woman pastor might be considered exemplary in many ways, St. Francis and Valerie Chapman continually face controversy. Some believe its mission to feed and assist the poor to be misguided and actually injurious. Gentrification has already begun in certain areas of Portland's southeast side. Shabby turn-of-the-century wood frame houses have been renovated and now glisten with fresh paint. The downward spiral that the area witnessed has abated and professionals are considering moving to the neighborhood. But some voices of change call out, who wants to live side-by-side with the homeless? Who wants their children to play side-by-side with sleeping vagrants in St. Francis Park, which covers nearly a city block just behind the church?

As Valerie and I stroll through the park one afternoon, we indeed find a peaceful oasis. The huge pond has been drained but hopefully will soon be filled again with water, which will further soften the sound of street traffic. On the edge of the pool, the words of St. Francis are artfully written in ceramic tile: *"Praised be my Lord God, with all of his creatures. For our Brother the Sun who brings us the day. For our Sister the Moon and for the stars set clear and lovely in heaven."*

"If the homeless drive away the residents or the residents drive away the homeless, we have failed," Valerie says. "This is not easy, to have the two live in some kind of harmony, but that is our mission. This is exactly where the Church needs to be, in the middle of difficult situations. And people come to St. Francis because they see that while we are not always successful, we are at least trying to reconcile the 'haves' and the 'have-nots.' This is not a church for everyone. Many Catholics who have been away for years find us a way back to the Church. Maybe we help them get a former marriage straightened out or show them that the Church really does care about them, regardless of where their lives have taken them. They stay for a while, then they go back to a parish nearer where they live. That's fine; they have come home."

One of the people who found St. Francis her pathway to Catholicism is Sandra Wilde, a fifty-two-year-old educator and recent convert. "I had—and have—a lot of disagreements with the Church on gender and reproductive issues, but as I searched many churches and even some New Age stuff, I found this was the place I wanted to be. I had found a church that was big enough for me—with my feminism and open mind."

I walk around the St. Francis neighborhood and see men sleeping peacefully on what passes for the parish lawn. In the parish offices, I sit in a once-grand living room that now houses cast-off, 50s-era mismatched tables and a leatherette sofa; a musty smell rises up from rugs that hold an aromatic history of this place. I listen as Valerie checks in with her children and makes sure her daughter carefully reads the questions on the placement test she is about to take. It is easy to both fall in love with this place and at the same time realize that it would not be the parish of many a Catholic's dreams.

As I help sort mail one morning, it becomes evident to me that the men and women for whom St. Francis is the only home they know live a life of turmoil and chaos. Some letters they receive demand urgent replies; others, unclaimed, are from loved ones with postmarks many months old. Yet this parish, led by a single mother of six and infused with the commitment of laypeople, willingly lives with that chaos. Most of the parishioners do not worry about their next meal or where they will sleep, but they have agreed to live in that crucible where the lofty words of the gospel meet the demands of the world and, as their mission statement proclaims: "to reach out rather than build a safe place to be."

St. Francis of Assisi

861 North Socora
Wichita, Kansas 67212
(316) 722-4404
www.stfranciswichita.com

✦ POINTS OF EXCELLENCE: ✦

1. Stewardship—Time and Talent First

2. Eucharistic Adoration—Seeds of Contemplation

3. Catholic Education—and Free

This parish provides a free elementary school education for all its children, and when those children graduate, the parish pays the tuition at the regional Catholic high school. Weekly attendance at the Sunday liturgies hovers at 85 percent, and no one budges until the servers extinguish the last candle. Over three hundred people attend weekday Mass—not including the school children. This parish has no second collections or bingo, yet its income not only takes care of the parish's needs, but also helps other Catholic churches in the area. It supports a free medical clinic for the working poor, providing everything from heart valve replacements to amoxicillin for a baby's infected ear. It's a parish where perpetual adoration of the blessed sacrament has been observed for over a decade.

Time warp? A remembrance of pre–Vatican II days? A fairy-tale parish set in a sort of Catholic Oz, where everything is perfect?

Well, St. Francis of Assisi is in Dorothy's Kansas, and while not everything is perfect in Wichita, this parish provides a stunning example of what happens when a young priest with a vision at once simple and profound, modern and biblical takes seriously what had always been considered a Protestant concept. In the process, he transformed not only a parish, which great priests can certainly do, but also the entire diocese in which he serves.

The story of this parish, like some of the others discussed in this book, started on a less than encouraging note. Father Thomas McGread was assigned to St. Francis in 1968. A newly formed parish of six hundred families, it presented all the expected challenges, such as construction of a school and sanctuary. But St. Francis had other, deeper problems. Factionalism reigned. Vatican II had recently concluded, and it seemed as if each parishioner had a personal vision for implementing the council. St. Francis had seen three pastors come and three pastors go in less than two years. It was considered a priest's graveyard. Father McGread was told that if he could not or did not want to continue after a six-month trial period, he would be reassigned with no questions asked.

The last of six children from a family in the north of Ireland, Tom McGread had been trained to work in the missionary field, since Ireland had a surplus of priests at the time. His vocation took him from the potato fields and rolling hills of Country Tyrone to the wheat fields of flat-as-a-table central Kansas. Although an unexpected post, he came with his love for the Church and his priesthood and brought along his forgiving nature. Here he discovered a concept almost totally alien to Catholics of the time: stewardship.

Stewardship is the biblical directive to treat all abilities, good fortune and material means as gifts from God. Those who happened to receive them should consider them as little more than on loan and should use them wisely and with gratitude. While tithing, the biblical benchmark of donating 10 percent of one's crops or wealth—or in more modern terms, of a paycheck—was part of the stewardship plan, many found it an idealistic concept. Few Catholic pastors in their right mind would ever propose it to their congregations.

Whether in his right mind or not, Father McGread wanted to do exactly that. He had read of the work of

✦ 1. STEWARDSHIP—TIME AND TALENT FIRST ✦

The "stewardship way of life" has produced a parish that provides both free education for its own and social outreach into Wichita's inner city, but something has happened in individual lives far beyond such material manifestations. Parishioners began to see a difference in their lives. I heard, over and over again, how the biblical promise of a hundredfold return has held true.

"It's not about business," says Paul Eck, "that if I give this much to God, he's going to give me that much in return. It's about a satisfaction deep inside that you are being generous with a God who has been generous to you."

At St. Francis the eventual target is the biblical tithe—10 percent, with 8 percent allotted to the parish and 2 percent to other charities. Most people start off with a much smaller proportion of their treasure but, like Paul Eck, they find that as they give more they do not miss the money and even enjoy the process. "You get ten times or a hundred times back in satisfaction, the good feeling that you are a part of something that educates kids, helps the poor, takes care of parishioners' needs and helps to increase a spiritual life. What better place to put your money than something like that?"

Fathers Joseph Jennings and David Sultan in Mobile, Alabama, who promoted stewardship as not so much a financial but a spiritual pursuit, and it made complete sense to him. It was a matter of need.

When one speaks of "need" in today's Catholic Church, most often the needs of the parishioners come to mind—support groups after divorce, psychological counseling, day care for children. For Father McGread, need proved more basic; it was embedded in the very soul of every person.

"People have the need to give," he says, as we sit at the dining room table in the spacious rectory at St. Francis. He is, as the Irish might say, a fine cut of a man, with a full head of white hair, a ready laugh and a kindly if raspy voice punctuated by an intermittent cough from a bit too much smoking. It is an incongruous scene, this ruddy seventy-one-year-old Irishman in Roman collar and black suit sitting in a gorgeous ultramodern two-level rectory with an exposed stairway at the center of the living room leading up to the bedrooms on the second floor. He might have Old World values, but when he built in the New World, he built well.

"If they didn't have this need, nothing of what we do would work; it would be false. But people at their heart are good, generous, and when they are faced with their many blessings, want to share that with others."

He smiles, showing well-spaced teeth, his eyes closing just a bit to show his utter belief and delight in what he is prepared to say. "If I would have started with asking people to give more money or to tithe, I would have lost half of them just mentioning those words. No, no," he says, shaking his head. "*Strdship* (his wonderful pronunciation) begins with the *time* and *talent* parts of the time, talent and treasure we hear so much about. Once people invest themselves—their time and whatever talents they might have—the treasure comes naturally."

Of course, it did not prove so easy and did not come that quickly. "Oh, they didn't even look me in the eye the first few Sundays." But Father McGread, who has since been named a monsignor, was undaunted by the cool reception.

I later have breakfast at the Rolling Hills Country Club, where Monsignor McGread is a member. There he plays golf and works the locker room for both converts and fallen-away Catholics as well as offering opportunities to those outside his parish who might also have that need to give. There I learn a bit more about the process of introducing stewardship. It took a few years for enough people to see the value of stewardship to form a committee to bring the practice to the parish at large. Paul Eck tells of his own gradual conversion to the "*strdship*" (and it was so embedded in this native Kansan that he *did* pronounce it like that) way of life.

"I'm a hardheaded German who's not about to part with a buck unless I have to. I came from a parish that had pew rent, and money was raised by assessment, not out of the goodness of your heart. But with the monsignor I began to see it another way. I was a

Monsignor Thomas McGread

blessed man; why shouldn't I readily give back what was a gift to me? And a table with some food on it has a way of getting to people."

Paul is referring to the annual church dinner, catered and free of charge, that kicks off the yearly stewardship drive. At the dinner, various ministries report on what the parish does, and people like Paul and Betty Eck give testimony about embracing the stewardship way of life. Later, a ministry fair illustrates what activity might best suit each person's time and talent. Finally, there is an invitation ("always an invitation, never a demand or even a request," the monsignor underscores) to live their lives this way.

One parishioner, who owns a string of fast-food franchises, contributes $10,000 a month. A mother on welfare gives a few dollars when she can.

The Mass and Eucharist certainly comprise two of the focal points of the parish's spiritual life. Monsignor McGread's sermons deftly weave scripture with everyday problems; liturgies and music, while somewhat straightforward and unadorned (like a good, solid loaf of Kansas whole wheat bread) respond well to the community's needs. However, St. Francis has another major spiritual focus, one that might astonish any Catholic, regardless of his or her own approach to God.

For the past eleven years, seven days a week, twenty-four hours a day (except for Mass times), the parish has had perpetual adoration of the blessed sacrament in a small chapel just off the twelve-hundred-seat sanctuary. Monsignor McGread would not allow banks of vigil candles in the main church, because he wanted to wean people from what he considered sometimes superstitious practices. However, he eventually responded as more and more of them asked for perpetual adoration. "When something rises up from the people, you need to listen to it," he says.

The parish instituted the practice just as the American Bishops' liturgical committee began to discourage it. Despite that, it quietly continued. By recommending that the practice be discontinued, the bishops undoubtedly hoped to bring people out of privatistic pious practices so that they might gather together for the Eucharist. They wanted to encourage the formation of holistic communities, a people of God alive with the spirit of Vatican II, as opposed to so many aesthetes.

The people of St. Francis have managed to do both; they combined this ancient and sometimes out-of-favor practice with a churchgoing, communitarian congrega-

✦ 2. EUCHARISTIC ADORATION — SEEDS OF CONTEMPLATION ✦

Although periodic eucharistic adoration services had always been part of St. Francis, more and more people began coming to Monsignor McGread asking for something more. Out of this outpouring of desire came perpetual adoration of the blessed sacrament, which has continued for over eleven years. Dan Loughman, a self-acknowledged workaholic who admits he doesn't spend enough time on his spiritual life, has read St. John of the Cross, St. Therese of Lisieux, and Thomas à Kempis during his hours in the small chapel. Other hard-charging businessmen and women—as well as harried parents of young children—find their hour of silence the best hour of their week. Rarely is the person who signed up to be present alone. Because the chapel is open at all hours, it encourages those short visits that many people find is exactly what they need—at whatever hour they need them. "My wife and I have come at midnight on Wednesday for years," says Paul Eck. "Without it, an important part of our lives would be missing; we look forward to it."

tion. During my visit to St. Francis, I stop into the chapel at odd hours and find a rich mixture of people there: a mother reading the Bible and her daughter, who looks to be about ten, perusing a book of the saints; a young man with moussed hair and a college-professor type with a beard; a Generation-X woman executive, her head bowed low, praying the rosary.

They have an attractive, quiet space. On one side a glass wall overlooks the sanctuary; on the other is a wall of rust-colored Kansas sandstone, the primary building material of the church. Before them stands the monstrance. Statues of Mary, the Infant of Prague and St. Joseph, a picture of the Sacred Heart and vigil lights complete the scene. They read from bibles, the diocesan newspaper, a book they have brought along or one chosen from the table at the rear.

When I go to the chapel in the predawn hours on Sunday morning, I find a man wearing a Cozumel T-shirt and his wife, her hair tastefully dyed to a rich auburn but still mussed in the back. She had obviously risen quickly to come here for what I would find was "their hour."

"The phone doesn't ring; the kids aren't here with their requests," says Jelene Grady, a forty-seven-year-old mother of five. "I look forward to it all week. Here I know I will have an hour of peace, an hour with God and nothing can get in the way of that. Even in church you're looking around; here there are no distractions."

"Without this," says her husband, Dennis, "my week wouldn't be complete. It's a chance to examine exactly who you are, to see how you're living your life, what you need to do differently or better."

As I sit in the chapel one afternoon, I can almost hear the murmurs of all the prayers for help and of thanksgiving, for guidance and for strength that have wafted to heaven in those eleven years. I find a real presence there, a unifying power for the people of this church. Although unaware of the specific words and thoughts of all the others, each had felt their presence and been touched by God in this place of silence and prayer. Almost ten years ago, Jeff Fashing prayed here about getting married; the year before last he was ordained a priest. Surely God has pointed the people of St. Francis in other directions as well.

While Monsignor McGread developed his at once simple and yet quite sophisticated approach to stewardship, he also built upon what he considers the three legs of any good parish: prayer, service and hospitality. Prayer at St. Francis is the prayer of the Church, the Mass, as well as individual prayer, nurtured in the adoration chapel. His personal prayer life includes the daily Office of the Hours. He has worn out four sets of breviaries, and the fifth looks well used. The once silken tabs that mark the various sections are but stubs of faded cloth.

Service has taken on many different forms. When he heard of widows buying more funeral than they really needed, wanted or could afford because of the "soft-sell" techniques of some funeral directors, he began to accompany them to make the arrangements. He pointed out that indeed dear Charles might have liked mahogany but the simpler pine or birch casket would hold him just as well. When one funeral director dug in his heels, the monsignor threatened to have the body moved before nightfall. They quickly reached an agreement, and word got around the city. Soon, price enhancement was squelched.

Even when even random callers appear at the church, Monsignor McGread readily receives them. He offers advice on real estate brokers or mortgage companies, the right college or the best therapist. The monsignor always seems to have an answer and happily makes the first phone call if ice needs breaking. "We are in the service industry; isn't that pretty clear?" he asks rhetorically.

As for hospitality, new members are warmly greeted in person. They are not given collection envelopes, but rather a packet of information outlining the seventy-odd ministries they might participate in, immediately sweeping them into the busy St. Francis family. Monsignor McGread also sees to it that the parish's hospitality consists of a lot of small, personal acts. When Matt Gear, a notorious "bad boy," was about to be kicked out of his school, Monsignor McGread accepted him into the St. Francis elementary school, sensing that a change in venue was what the boy needed. Matt currently attends St. Mary's College in Winona, Minnesota, in a preseminary program. If he continues to ordination, he will join the thirteen men and women the parish has launched into religious life. Three more are currently in the seminary.

A young woman in a difficult, abusive marriage came to Monsignor McGread seeking advice. Prac-

✦ 3. CATHOLIC EDUCATION — AND FREE ✦

At St. Francis of Assisi a Catholic education is a right, not a privilege. All children of parishioners can attend grades K through 12 for free. The parish asks parents to give of their time, talents and treasure, both to the school and the parish at large. While parents—and all parishioners—are encouraged to tithe, no one applies any pressure to donate a certain amount. For instance, a single mother on welfare might donate only a few dollars to the parish during certain periods of her life. Other parents and even those without children in the schools may give more. "I've offered, for those who choose not to live the stewardship way of life, to just pay the tuition, which is about $2,500 a year right now," says Monsignor McGread. "I've never had a taker." Teachers in the school receive wages almost at public-school levels and the faculty and staff are stable, indicating that St. Francis of Assisi School is a good place to teach.

ticing his understanding of proper Christian hospitality, he didn't recite the standard "until death do you part" discursion. He told her that if, for her own sake and sanity and that of her two children, she had to live apart, then she should do so. He also said her children would remain at St. Francis, regardless of what she could pay. Her children are now grown, and she has earned a master's degree, "and without Catholic schooling and the monsignor's support, I don't know if I would have made it," she says. "It was a rocky road, but my kids have values and morals, the greatest gifts they could ever have to take them into life. There were years when I could contribute to the church and years I couldn't; monsignor never put any pressure on me. I was one of the family, and he was with me."

"Be kind," this wise pastor advises as we walk about the St. Francis grounds one afternoon. "People will forgive you for just about anything if you're kind to them." On a recent Sunday, after one of his two young curates chastised a group of teenage boys standing in the back of the church, the monsignor in turned chastised the curate. "After all, they were in church, weren't they? You could just go up and stand with them for a moment. They'd get the idea. You don't

Presentation of the gifts

always have to be telling people what they're doing wrong. They don't like it much and they don't learn to love unless you show them love first."

When told about seven-year-old Alison, who has dreamed of being a priest since she was a toddler, raising her hands with an imaginary host and chalice at the consecration, Monsignor McGread just grins. "You never know," he says, only to be one-upped by the curate. "Don't confuse her," he snaps, indicating that such youthful ambition should be squelched.

"People don't come to church to be beaten up," Monsignor McGread says. "There is enough of that out in the world. I try to take people where they are, not where we think they ought to be. They'll get there if we only give them a chance. They want to come to a place where they are accepted and respected, a place of common values, a place of solidarity."

St. Francis has a slightly conventional feel to it; some might even consider it to have more of a conservative bent, with not a copy of *The National Catholic Reporter* in sight, but stacks of *Our Sunday Visitor* and the *National Catholic Register* (even a few copies of the ultra-traditionalist *Wanderer*, placed there by an adamant and righteous parishioner, the monsignor says) at the rear of the church. But it is a place of shared values. Dogma and doctrine are not the first considerations here; involvement is. "Yes, I would say our people agree with the Pope on just about everything, but they're too busy helping other people to worry much about that sort of thing."

When teaching the children about the Eucharist and transubstantiation, Monsignor McGread advises against telling them that it is the body and blood of Christ. "They'll get sick to their stomachs. I tell them the host is the love of Christ; that they can understand."

While the parish might not stand at the forefront of social activism, it believes in and practices care and help for the less fortunate. Our Lady of Guadelupe clinic, which serves some 2,500 of the working poor each year, provides but one example of that kind of social outreach and a good illustration of Monsignor McGread's ingenious ability to channel people's need to share their bounty.

Some fifteen years ago, Dr. Daniel Tatpati, a physician born and trained in India, heard a National Public Radio report describing how the working poor were denied medical help because they were neither wealthy enough to afford private health insurance nor poor enough to qualify for Medicaid coverage. He wanted to start a modest clinic in the St. Francis elementary school. The monsignor, pointing out that he could serve far more of the working poor in downtown Wichita, helped Dr. Tatpati find a home for his clinic, as well as initial funding. When that funding ran out, the monsignor promised that St. Francis would stand behind the clinic and keep it open.

"We have the best general practitioners and specialists in Wichita giving a few hours a week, hospitals that will take care of our patients and pharmacies that give medicines either free or at cost," Dr. Tatpati tells me as we stand in the church after ten o'clock Mass. "Doctors are very willing to give those hours at the clinic and, if needed, see a few—we don't overburden them—patients in their office. All we have to do is ask; whether or not they are members here, they believe in stewardship too. But the funny thing is that we have so many willing volunteers, I sometimes can't even get on the schedule to donate my time!"

Dr. Tatpati recently volunteered his services for a heart-valve replacement the total cost of which would have been upward of $35,000. When an eye surgeon and local hospital agreed to do a cornea transplant for free, Dr. Tatpati needed only to arrange funds for the cornea itself, which bore a $1,600 price tag. A phone call explaining how the other services had been donated brought a free cornea to Wichita. "Why do I do it?" Dr. Tatpati repeats a question. "It makes me feel so darn good."

Because of Monsignor McGread's outstanding success at weaving stewardship into the fabric of his parish—and then spreading the stewardship way of life to the Wichita diocese —other parishes and dioceses have asked him to come and teach them about his methods.

"But most of them miss the point," he says. "They go right to the treasure part; they see the money our people give, and they want to take a shortcut right to it. Can't be done. They miss the fact that people have to undergo a conversion to the stewardship way of life and that it is gradual and that they have to feel it is their decision to make. People have to feel a sense of ownership in the parish. When they know it's theirs—not the priest's—and that they are the real force behind everything, they want to give of themselves—again, in time, in talent and then in treasure.

"I hear from priests that they are too busy to undertake a true stewardship program. They don't realize that everything they already do will fit under this umbrella, that they will actually have more hands to do the work once people are on board. Dioceses hire development directors, financial types, to raise money. This is about faith, not finance. They miss the point.

"There are no obvious rewards for the *strdship* way of life," the monsignor says as I end my visit. "But the change in people's attitude about life—you see that right away."

Monsignor McGread's approach to stewardship has gradually spread throughout the diocese of Wichita. Its ninety parishes practice stewardship—some more successfully than others—and all of its thirty-two elementary schools are free. Other parishes, from Florida to Colorado, have incorporated the approach, and the ripple effect continues. When Hewlett-Packard moved St. Francis parishioner Chris Wiggins to the Boston area, the pastor of his new church called him in and asked point blank why he gave so much in the collection. "I come from a stewardship parish," he said with more than a little pride.

As my plane lifts off the ground and banks out over the Kansas wheat fields that stretch 360 degrees in uniform square plots to the horizon, I gaze down on a part of the country that seems to triumph in uniformity. Even the lay of the land seems too orderly, where 640-acre sections were once parceled out to pioneers heading West.

Yet that land is being divided, fought over and farmed by both families and agribusiness. On those plains live welfare mothers with little left over at the end of the week and executives who can afford to give thousands of dollars a week. There are all of the complexities and hurts of life that one finds on the East or West Coast. That mother of two, whose children were educated at St. Francis, was crushed when other mothers stigmatized her for being a divorcée and wouldn't let their daughters ride with her on a field trip. Lack of charity—small-mindedness—is part of life here, as anywhere.

For her and so many others, however, there is an island of hope, and stability. A pastor's acceptance has firmly stamped itself upon this rich land. Some 600 families, now grown to 2,500, have found that being good stewards can bring them happiness beyond what they give or what they receive. A certain attitude, a habit of being, has infused their lives. They function in ways strikingly similar to the first Christian communities—giving according to their means; receiving according to that which they require. I have the feeling that as the Church moves, St. Francis will move with it, for it is traditional in the best sense without being mindlessly traditionalistic.

St. Mark's

7503 Northview
Boise, Idaho 83704
(208) 375-6651
www.cyberhighway.net/~stmarks/

+   POINTS OF EXCELLENCE: +

1. Welcoming Committee Visits

2. Evangelization Retreats—the Power of Faith Sharing

3. Reaching Teenagers

Stories are often told within church circles of an inspired pastor coming to a parish and infusing it with new life. In Father Steve Rukavina's case, it worked the other way around.

Father Rukavina got word of his transfer to St. Mark's in Boise, Idaho, at a time when his vocation had begun to feel tired and somewhat uninspired. While he still loved being a priest, he had been worn down by the constant demands of weekly Masses, funerals, weddings, committee meetings, internal bickering, peacekeeping and the maintenance of a physical plant. At the time, he served as the pastor of a somewhat typical six-hundred-family parish. The parishioners respected and admired him—and looked to him to do pretty much *everything*. Father Rukavina is the first to admit that he isn't that broadly talented.

Upon his arrival at St. Mark's, he found a vibrant parish with an incredibly high level of lay participation, yet which had once suffered the spiritual ennui he knew all too well. St. Mark's had been built in the mid-1970s to serve the Catholics moving to Boise's west side. Idaho's largest city and a desirable location because of its breathtaking setting and strong economic base, Boise was not a Catholic bastion. Catholics make up only 15 percent of its 275,000 people.

St. Mark's had mirrored the city's growth in its first twenty years, steadily increasing in membership. While no crisis required a corporate examination of conscience within the church community, something bubbled just below the surface. It bubbles imperceptibly, I think, beneath the surface of many parishes.

A number of the parishioners felt that they were not yet the people of God that they could be. It was something between a nonspecific need and an aching longing. "I was searching, but not really understanding what

I was searching for," Barbara Monihan says. The people of St. Mark's viewed the church as their spiritual home, the place where people attended Mass, were baptized, married and buried. But, they wondered, how might the parish be more a part of their everyday life? How might religious belief become a living, breathing presence? How might well-intentioned Catholics go to a deeper level? How might devotionalism be transformed into an abiding spirituality?

When parishioner Linda Konkol returned from a visit to California, she thought she had seen a way. There, in Visalia, a series of parish retreats had transformed Holy Family parish. But the retreats were not the only reason why Linda described Holy Family as "on fire." It was also the insertion of the retreatants into small Christian communities, which kept alive the flame from the weekend retreat experience.

Linda returned from that fateful trip to find what idealistic parishioners might hope for, but seldom find: a pastor with a sufficiently intact ego to allow such a lay-driven initiative to take root. Father John Donoghue, who retired when Father Rukavina and Father Len MacMillan were assigned to the growing parish as copastors, wanted to find out what the program was all about. In December 1992 he went to Visalia and made the retreat.

"I'd been a priest for forty years and I'd never seen anything like it," he says. "The way people shared their lives—it was just fantastic. No one is the same after that weekend. I wasn't. This was a place where you got your bell rung." Coming from the distinguished-looking, white-haired priest, this was high praise. "I was determined we were going to do this at St. Mark's and do it that very spring."

He and parishioner Pat Ott set to work. Seventeen members of Holy Family as well as their pastor, Father Mike LaStere, drove the 650 miles to Boise to assist in the first retreat. It proved to be a huge success.

The effort succeeded not only because the time was right for planting this seed at St. Mark's—the timely work of grace or inspiration of the Holy Spirit—but also because the parish had, even if unconsciously, prepared the soil. The parish council had studied the papal encyclical *Evangelization of Peoples* and agreed upon certain goals for their own parish renewal. These included a more intense experience of Jesus, outreach to unchurched and fallen-away Catholics and the fostering of small communities.

They had also vowed to visit every home in the parish to ask people what they needed or wanted to pray about and to see how the parish could better meet their needs. In one month, eighty-two teams of two people visited all twelve hundred households in the parish. They found both a spiritual hunger for God and a yearning for true, deep human community.

That first retreat proved a crucial initial step in "converting" the parishioners of St. Mark's. On a spring morning, some six years and twenty-one retreats later, the thirty colorful banners proudly paraded through the St. Mark's sanctuary give testi-

✦ 1. WELCOMING COMMITTEE VISITS ✦

When people register at St. Mark's, they are visited — usually within a week—by members of the Welcoming Committee. The point of this visit is not to find out what the new member can do for the parish but what the parish can do for them. They ask generally if the new parishioner has any needs, and then get down to specifics: Does the family have teenagers, elderly relatives, young adults? They answer questions about the Evangelization Retreat, tell of their own experiences and give the dates of the next retreats. They explain that it is a quick way to be a part of the parish community, but in a nonthreatening and noncoercive manner. They leave their own phone numbers if the person might later have questions. They try to show with their enthusiasm what the parish has meant in their own lives, but they do it calmly and positively. They make it clear they are there to inform, not to get some sort of commitment. It is a friendly visit, neighbor to neighbor, to welcome a new person or family.

mony to the parishwide conversion. Each spiritual coat of arms represents one of the small faith communities that has transformed St. Mark's from within. Handmade by members of the communities, each banner is unique—"Hearts on Fire" portrays golden flames bursting from crimson hearts; "God's Little Challenges" has an angel surrounded by golden rays; and "Footsteps to Jesus" shows footprints leading up a winding path to Jesus.

Over a thousand St. Mark's parishioners had already experienced one of these retreats. Hundreds remained active in these small faith communities, which had done everything from welcoming refugees from Kosovo to supplying dozens of RCIA sponsors to recruiting three hundred volunteers when a planning committee needed help for a new sanctuary. St. Mark's had come alive and people spoke of newfound spiritual depths they never dreamed existed.

During our visit to St. Mark's another weekend retreat was about to begin. Some thirty-nine people had signed up; twenty leaders were ready to guide them. While attending the retreat, Parish/Congregation Study researcher Melanie Bruce experienced what many have found in the variety of encounter weekends that have swept—and continue to sweep—across the Catholic landscape. The Cursillo movement in the 1950s was the first widespread initiative in our time to encourage the spirituality of laypeople and to foster their beliefs through shared prayer, spiritual reading and discussion. Beginning in the 1970s, Father John McDermott's Cornerstone Retreats at Presentation parish in Upper Saddle River, New Jersey, built upon the Cursillo experience, emphasizing the telling of "faith stories" so that attendees could see both the difficulties and the rewards of leading an attentive spiritual life.

✦ 2. EVANGELIZATION RETREATS— THE POWER OF FAITH SHARING ✦

The guidelines for St. Mark's evangelization retreats—which are held three or four times a year—come from Holy Family in Visalia, California, one of the pioneers in this movement.* The parish generates interest through a print publicity campaign and by having people who have attended previous retreats tell their own faith stories before each of the weekend liturgies. "This validates what that person in the pew is already thinking, much better than a priest getting up there to tell them why they should come," says Father Steve Rukavina. Central to the success of the retreats is the telling of those stories, which often includes experiences common to many retreatants, and then the insertion of those retreatants into small faith groups. There the enthusiasm and community engendered during the retreat can continue to infuse the person's life. In today's ever more mobile society, the ability to be part of an instant family through small faith communities not only roots people in the church, but within a group of caring friends.

*Another parish that successfully used evangelization retreats, developed by Father John McDermott, is the Church of the Presentation in Upper Saddle River NJ (Phone: 201-327-1313 [Web site: www.churchofpresentation.org]). For Hispanics, the SINE program (*Sistema Integral Nueva Evangelization),* started by Father Alfonso Navarro, has been particularly effective (Web site: http://spin.com.mx/~raulma/inicio-i.html).

He was not alone; other condensed spiritual encounters were fashioned to meet the unchanging need every soul feels for kinship with God, while tailoring the message for modern sensibilities. A key component of the RENEW program (www.renewintl.org), an innovative approach founded by Father Thomas Kleissler and used by hundreds of parishes in America and abroad, underscores weekend retreats as the crucial hinge in parishwide revivification. Small faith communities assure continuing education and support as well as provide the base for incorporating faith into the home, the workplace, the world itself.

St. Mark's in Boise follows the model it brought back from Visalia. The parish charges nothing to attend and provides all meals. Each evangelization retreat lasts from 5 P.M. Friday until 4 P.M. Sunday. When retreatants enter the St. Mark's gym on Friday afternoon, they find a small highly polished stone and a card on each seat. The card reads, "I will remove from your body the heart of stone and give you a heart of flesh" (Ezek 36:26). Upbeat music and songs led by a nine-piece band keep the retreat moving and about once an hour, a church member offers a testimony. This is followed by small-group prayer and discussion. Throughout the weekend, retreatants are asked to reaffirm the basic elements of the Catholic faith. They renew their baptismal vows, participate in a "laying on of hands" ceremony at the church altar and pray the rosary en masse. During the retreat opportunities for the sacrament of reconciliation are offered, the Liturgy of the Hours is reviewed, the reading of scripture is encouraged and practical tips for enriching one's prayer life are given. The attitude of the retreat leaders is always a gentle "Try this . . . you might like it," as opposed to "You *have* to do this to be a good Catholic."

The testimonies given by former retreatants are often wrenchingly personal, touching on such things as the death of a loved one, divorce, addiction, sexual promiscuity or debilitating illness. They reach deeply into their souls and share their life stories and their faith struggles. It is not uncommon to see tears running down the faces of the speakers and retreatants as well. The speakers display an amazing courage; and while their stories are unique, the message is the same: God's love and forgiveness know no bounds.

After the testimonies, the retreatants break down into smaller groups, sorted by age and sex. Group leaders encourage retreatants to speak in the first person and contribute their own faith stories. The accepting atmosphere strengthens the bond of trust, and many find the courage to share. Trust, acceptance and openness to the unfamiliar are somehow easy habits to acquire at the retreat.

"I was raised Pentecostal Holiness and I've seen things this weekend I never thought I'd see Catholics doing!" says one young man in T-shirt and jean shorts during the retreat's "open mike" comment period at the retreat researcher Melanie Bruce attended. He got a laugh, but many might agree. For example, many Catholics have never experienced the laying on of hands, a healing ceremony one often finds at charismatic events.

At the end of the retreat weekend, the participants enter St. Mark's darkened gym, transformed by a hundred glittering candles. Tables are covered with white cloths and laid with a simple meal of pasta salad. Soft instrumental music plays in the background. The candles and the carefully prepared meal say, "We love you and God loves you" louder and more poignantly than words could express.

In reply to a questionnaire, some people wrote of the retreat's strong influence even many years after they had experienced it. "It unlocked the Holy Spirit within me and helped me discover it in others. I invite people to attend a retreat and I tell them it will change their lives and their outlook toward religion forever," said one woman who had attended a retreat five years before. Another woman who had been a "habitual, complacent Catholic" before the retreat went through a "spiritual renewal that led me closer to our Lord and gave me a deeper appreciation of my faith. I'm now a committed Catholic and a member of a small faith community." One man said, "Mass became more meaningful for me. I came to believe in the real presence of Christ in the Eucharist—something I had struggled with my whole life." He had been to a retreat almost six years earlier. Indeed, St. Mark's parishioners tend to speak of their lives in terms of "before" and "after" the retreat.

When I return to St. Mark's, I speak to some people

who had been on the retreat two months earlier. What Dan Boespflug, a forty-three-year-old optometrist, relates might represent the experience of many others. "I had an elementary knowledge of Catholicism, the basics, I guess, but it never was enough for my life. I needed to hear about a God not only on the altar on Sunday, but a God whom I could take into my life, a God who understands that I am human, that I will make mistakes, a God who is always willing to forgive me. I came off a real high after the retreat and then I was dragging my heels about going to the small faith community each week. We're all tired, overcommitted people. But then when I go, I'm refreshed, reminded, supported. Small faith communities were the past of the Church and, from what I am experiencing in my life, they are the future as well."

"As the current pastors, we have hopefully added to this faith community, but we did not build it," says Father Rukavina, forty-eight. "The people built it. It's the difference between looking at a parish as the gas station where you can fill up once a week—if you come at all—to the parish as the hub for faith communities that deal with the nitty-gritty of life on a continuing basis, where people can talk about the deepest things in their lives, things they couldn't talk about anyplace else. In our society, where few of us have family living in the same town, with people moving all the time, the faith community provides an instant church family, a church within a church. Our feeling is: Why should people have to wait two or three years to get to know other wonderful members of the church?"

As St. Mark's evangelization coordinator, this is how Sally O'Keefe sees it: "The key to the lasting success of the retreats is that while people after the retreat are in orbit, they need the small communities as their reentry window. The steady, loving community provides a continuing grace for people to be active in their faith."

And now, St. Mark's is in a position to spread the word about the weekend retreats and small faith communities. Other parishes turn to them for help and St. Mark's retreat leaders have helped to start similar movements in other Oregon, Idaho and Nevada churches.

"*Evangelizing* is a word that Catholics, both laypeople and clergy, run from because they have images of 800 numbers to call with their credit card pledges, in-your-face demands, Jimmy Swaggert with sweat on his forehead and a Bible in his hand," says Father Rukavina. "If you are afraid of that word, you are choosing not to be Catholic," adds Father Donoghue. "Evangelization is the tip of the spear. Evangelization is taking your beliefs into the world and it is in the world that religious beliefs are lived out, in places priests never get to, where people are."

Father Len MacMillan had also experienced a crisis of faith before coming to St. Mark's; at times he even considered leaving the priesthood. The demands of parish ministry loomed large; the rewards seemed few and the loneliness was numbing. Now, as we sit in the

Prayer before Sunday liturgy

sun outside the rectory, a pleasant low-slung ranch-style house far from the church, he appears a happy and fulfilled man. "There is a certain kind of maturity about a parish like this, where laypeople have come into their own, where they are comfortable as both leaders and participants," he says. "Where they come up with ideas and never ask Father to implement them because they are ready to make them a reality. The line—the chasm—between priest and people is bridged; this is truly collaboration. Father Donoghue set up a church to run without him. We are the beneficiaries."

St. Mark's is known for more than its adult small faith communities. Once parents found new excitement both in being in church and in exploring their own deepening spirituality, they wanted the same for their children and grandchildren. Again, within the broadly diverse human community of the Catholic Church they found a new approach to involve young Catholics.

Life Teen originated in St. Timothy's Parish in Mesa, Arizona. While St. Mark's adopted this fresh approach, with its teen-driven liturgies, discussions, retreats and outreach, Father Donoghue and then Fathers Rukavina and MacMillan adapted it to the needs and nature of their own teenagers. Father Dale Fushek, the program's founder, dreamed that Life Teen would be a catalyst to invigorate the faith of Catholic teenagers. Many Life Teen programs meet that lively, youth-empowered vision, although some, implemented differently, tend toward a pietistic, highly dogmatic approach. Currently over six hundred parishes nationwide use variations of the techniques of the Life Teen program that has transformed Sunday evenings at St. Marks's.

"The real art in parish work does not always involve finding brand new approaches," says Father Rukavina. "Most of us just aren't that innovative. But if you look around there are usually ways that work if a parish is brave enough and open enough to try them. They can be adapted, shaped to fit a parish's needs. Life Teen is a perfect example."

When I attend a Life Teen liturgy on a hot, midsummer Sunday evening, I am amazed to see not only the number of teenagers in attendance, but also the number of adults, who also enjoy this fresh, relaxed, yet reverential liturgy. Teenagers plan the liturgy and serve as the leaders, readers, cantors and eucharistic ministers. At the consecration, when Father Rukavina raises first the host, then the chalice, a phalanx of teenagers with their arms intertwined around one another's

✦ 3. Reaching Teenagers ✦

When Father Steve Rukavina attended a Life Teen workshop at St. Timothy's Parish in Mesa, Arizona, he knew he had seen a powerful, effective way to reach and involve teenagers. He was not yet at St. Mark's, but he knew it was a program he wanted to implement. "Life Teen takes a major commitment from the whole parish, not only from the pastor; in fact he's a small part of it," Father Rukavina admits. For a yearly membership of $300, Life Teen headquarters sends out monthly packets that include liturgy planning guides, songs and suggestions for activities in the social hour called "Life Night" that follows the Life Teen liturgy. "You need to tailor the materials to your parish. We put in more catechesis, but we never cut short the social part—that's crucial. We had a semiformal dance that was extremely well attended, as was a swing-dancing lesson. We've taken a look at the songs, moving away from the 'me and Jesus' types—those with a lot of 'I's' in the lyrics to those with a more communal flavor, that 'we are young people moving together toward the kingdom.' We keep hearing that the youth are the future of the Church. Life Teen says they are the Church *today*; they have ownership *today*. That's the kind of spiritual maturity that is very appealing to young people, who are very sophisticated and don't want to be preached down to, or babied."

shoulders stand behind him. The crucifix that looms over their heads further adds to an extraordinarily impressive and powerful tableau: teenagers and their priest reverent yet comfortable in the presence of God and one another.

The liturgy ends with an upbeat version of "Awesome God," and congregants continue to sing and clap after the choir and five-piece Christian rock band (two CDs to their credit so far) have stopped. Lights are turned out to gently encourage the last people to leave. A popular Life Teen challenge goes, "The Mass never ends; it must be lived," and I leave with the distinct feeling that it would be. Preteens and younger children had eagerly participated, watching appealing role models on the altar whom they hope one day to emulate. "At St. Mark's you can be Catholic and proud of it," says Bryan Naugle, the twenty-three-year-old youth minister. "It's cool to be Catholic; it's cool to pray; it's cool to be reconciled, to be healed, to be with people who love you for what you are."

St. Mark's Life Teen liturgy draws teenagers not only from the parish but from across Boise. Mandi Davis, a somewhat typical teenager, wanted nothing to do with the Church as a fifteen-year-old. "My parents didn't go to church; I was in the Catholic high school, but under protest. Mass in my own parish was boring, and I always felt I was being preached at. On the suggestion of a friend who comes here, I went on a St. Mark's youth retreat a year ago. Wow!" Mandi's eyes widen. Her two-toned hair, the product of a bleach job growing out of her medium-length hair, shimmers as she shakes her head in disbelief. "I found great kids to be with, a church where I really felt accepted, priests that knew my name and cared about me, me personally. Sure, there are other voices in my life— 'let's go party' for sure—but now I come to church because I want to. I love being here."

As St. Mark's developed its "style"—and each excellent parish has its own—it found itself constantly having to adjust. "We are an accepting church," Father Rukavina tells me as we ride around Boise one day in his Ford Explorer, "but we also make demands. For instance, to merely baptize a child because people want the ritual, but have no concept of what it means and have no desire to raise that child in the Catholic-Christian tradition is nothing short of a sham." When one caller heard that parents needed to be registered for three months and understand their obligations in baptism, she asked, "Can you recommend another church that doesn't take this all so seriously?"

"We do take it seriously," says Father Rukavina. "At first communion both parents and children sign commitments, and the kids have to be able to recite the act of contrition, which the parents have taught them."

"We're not trying to be tough guys about it," says Father Len, who happens to have the chiseled chest and biceps of a disciplined weight lifter, "but these are opportunities for true grace if the individuals involved can be helped to see it. And these are times in people's lives when conversion can take place. How many

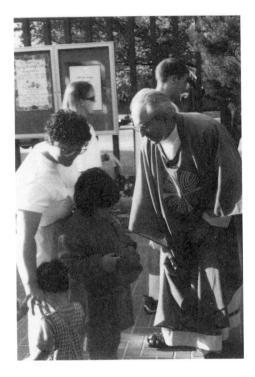

*Father Steve
Rukavina*

times do people come back to the church or start
to take it seriously after a meaningful baptism or a
wedding? And, actually, people want demands made
of them, but they also want to be treated as human
beings in the process."

The copastorate of Fathers Rukavina and MacMillan
is a source of amazement to anyone who knows them
at all well. Father Rukavina's idea of exercise is putter-
ing in his flowerbeds; Father Macmillan's, a good,
sweaty workout doing bench presses with a few hundred pounds. Father MacMillan is a neatnik; Father
Rukavina would never be so accused. But both have a

rich sense of humor. When a dinner prepared by the two priests was auctioned off for a winning bid of $5,000, they wanted to provide more than good food, so they served the meal dressed in togas, laurel leaves around their heads.

As they serve this 2,400-family church, they share a real affinity for the parish. They collaborate on homilies, so that the same basic message gets out at all the Masses. They plan ahead so homilies are not the frantic inspiration of early Sunday panic, but have continuity. This year their theme involves helping parishioners to see themselves as the Church beyond church walls. "We constantly try to go to another level," says Father Rukavina. "If you stand still, satisfied with your successes, the stagnation has already begun."

Both Father Steve and Father Len came from those archetypal midsized, one-priest parishes that comprise the vast majority of assignments within today's Church. And, with the declining number of ordained priests available and an ever increasing number of Catholics, the number of such parishes will continue to climb. While acknowledging the shortage of ordained clergy, the church finds itself at the center of a debate. Should ever-larger churches be formed from a consortium of smaller parishes so that this smaller pool of priests can serve more people? Or through using lay leaders, should the size of parishes be kept smaller and more personal?

"I certainly would not advocate for megaparishes," says Father Len, "but a parish where there is only one priest is a parish that is both blessed and limited by that one person. In a parish this size, with two priests and so many laypeople involved, I have a richer ministry because I'm not so spread out and diluted.

"What we work on is to allow many little churches to form within the larger church. If we are a big church, I hope to our people it at least feels small."

Final Thoughts

A reasonable question might be asked after all these parish visits. When all is said and done: What is the best Catholic parish in America?

I thought about that question often during my parish travels, and I think about it once again as I write these final words. Each time I come up with the same answer.

There is no "best" parish.

While all the parishes in this book are exemplary in many ways and each has its own unique flavor, none is perfect. None should be named "best." Each parish continues the process of becoming a place of refuge and welcome, a spiritual fountain where the thirsty might drink, a replica of the kingdom of God on earth. They are—as are all of us—on a pilgrimage that never ends, one that is always incomplete, imperfect.

If I were asked to construct the "best" parish, I might take the powerful stewardship of St. Francis in Wichita, the life-changing work with teenagers at St. Mark's in Boise, the neighborhood transformation of St. Peter Claver in New Orleans, the hunger for social justice and compassion of St. Francis in Portland, the excellent adult education of Holy Family in Inverness, Illinois, the soaring beauty of Our Lady Help of Christians' renovation in Newton, Massachusetts, the embracing sense of community in the Minnesota Catholic Area Parishes, the power of lay involvement in El Paso and combine them all into a single, magnificent parish.

That is possible to do on paper but, of course, no one could really join such a virtual parish. A seeker after such a perfect place would spend all of his or her time on an airplane, commuting from city to town in order to savor the many wonderful offerings these various parishes present. But it *is* possible to learn from them, to respectfully loot their treasury of experiences, practices, programs, approaches.

Creating an excellent parish surely takes some talent, but more importantly it requires trust both in people and in God. Mistakes will be made. Great parishes do some things well; they also stumble and sometimes fail miserably. But when a pastor and parish staff basically trust and like the people they deal with (I know this sounds too elementary to even mention, but it is sadly true that parishioners are too often considered annoyances, not cocreators of God's kingdom on earth), wonderful things naturally happen.

Excellent parishes regard parishioners as Jay Gatsby did his friend in that famous portrayal from F. Scott Fitzgerald's classic, *The Great Gatsby*: " . . .understood you as you would like to believe in yourself. . . .and had precisely the impression of you that, at your best, you hoped to convey." So it is in these excellent parishes: They see and seek the best in everyone.

What the vast majority of Catholic parishes in our country lack is not priests or resources, but vision, energy and hope. It is not an oppressive Church structure that hampers them; it is not an uninvolved laity that restricts them. The majority of our parishes are simply not reading the signs of the times. While this may seem a highly secularized culture, its very fragmentation, mobility and institution-averse nature find their antidote in the Catholic parish. Here one may find built-in community, acceptance, safety, growth and spirituality. Here is a path to God, to holiness and true happiness, both in tending to one's needs and those of others.

Vision. Energy. Hope. Despite the small number of clergy and shaky finances, vision is always possible for those brave enough to open their eyes to the spiritual hunger so evident in our day; energy is an untapped resource for those willing to feed their souls regularly; and hope awaits those who honestly believe that the God they claim to worship is indeed with them.

An excellent parish is not swayed by the latest ecclesiastical trends, a slave to test-marketed diocesan programs, or at the mercy of the so-called experts and consultants with fancy flip charts and reams of data. I have found that great parishes often emerge and succeed *in spite* of the planners—because they have the wisdom to look to people, not to the institution, to save them.

Today's parishes differ vastly from those of even a generation ago, and the parishes a generation from now will be transformed even more dramatically. Barring a miraculous increase in priestly vocations, the future of Catholicism—and, with it, the tried-and-true parish structure—seems to rest with laypeople. The 30,000 Catholic lay men and women currently in some sort of ministerial training dwarfs the 3,400 men who now populate our major seminaries. Overall and without counting those in formal training, this generation represents the best-educated group of Catholic laypeople in history. They have an unbelievable array of talents. They want to give of themselves to something beyond their own comfort or material success. They want a moral legacy for their children.

However, they will no longer attend churches that do not speak to their souls and their minds. Institutional loyalty ("once a Catholic, always a Catholic") doesn't have the strength it once did. Many cradle Catholics have gone to other religious denominations to feed their spiritual selves. Sadly, more have simply opted out of any religious practice. Additionally, a "silent major-ity" within Catholicism, those who belong to a parish and attend weekly Mass, are little more than Catholics by name, having found little impetus to bring religious beliefs into their real life. Young people and a huge and growing number of immigrants, many Hispanic, are not being reached. The Catholic Church will lose them unless more parishes, pastors and, increasingly, lay staff expose them to the transforming power and the attrac-tive lifestyle that Catholicism offers.

Beyond being excellent, each of the eight parishes I have profiled—and the hundreds more at the back of this book—have something to say not only to the Church, but to their communities and this country at large: a message, for example, about the power of community in rural Minnesota, spiritual aesthetics in Newton, Massachusetts, transformative adult spiritual enrichment in Inverness, Illinois, neighborhood renewal in New Orleans. These Catholic parishes are beacons of hope—not only for their people, but also far, far beyond.

What I saw in these excellent parishes amazed me. But I felt frustrated. "Why don't other parishes know about this?" I found myself asking. "Why don't they try these ways? They work so well." In the next section, I summarize the essential qualities of these parishes. In doing so, I hope these exemplary parishes inspire oth-ers. And I hope that seminarians and priests, nuns, lay men and women—those already in Church work and those in training—might spend time in these places.

Great parishes exist throughout the country; one of them is close to you. Although this might sound a bit preposterous, I would advocate visiting these sites, a sort of religious "freedom trail," for these are holy places, and having once visited, the pilgrims will never be the same. They will see how powerful an attitude of acceptance and service can be. Men and women need to experience great parishes in this country. In doing so they can encounter fresh insights and other visions of the Church and realize that their own dreams are not impossible.

When Peter Maurin and Dorothy Day founded the Catholic Worker movement, their goal, as Peter Maurin summarized it, was "creating places where it is easy to be good." This is *exactly* what parishes should be about. This could be the very first line in their mission statements. It has nothing to do with size or location or resources.

Much of what I have highlighted throughout this book is possible to do in most parishes with appropriate adjustments for size and resources. I don't suggest a parish undertake wholesale all that has been written about on these pages. That would not only be impossible, but—again, using the metaphor of a pilgrimage or journey—it would be like trying to take several trails at once.

The idea is to scan the horizon, to inventory both the needs and resources of those in the pews on Sunday and those just over the next low hill who are looking for companions with whom they might travel through life, and then to take the first step, trusting that God, as promised so many years ago, is truly present. The glow from this new spirit will quickly spread throughout the parish and beyond its walls as well.

Common Traits of
Excellent Parishes

These traits are offered as encouragement to parishes across America because some of these qualities are already in evidence in many parishes. And, for those parishes that seek true excellence, these traits are suggested as components of a model for the days head.

I have gathered these somewhat eclectic characteristics under the headings of approach, institutional life, community, the work, *and* spirituality.

APPROACH

1. Are Looked Upon as Missionary Outposts

Wherever they are located—in the suburbs, the city, a rural area or small town—excellent parishes essentially see themselves as missionary outposts. Catholicism has never existed without being in conflict with the prevailing culture; these parishes face that conflict directly and attempt to sanctify it. These parishes take time to understand the culture they are within and seek to meet the needs of the indigenous people whom they will serve. What are the community's needs, dreams, folkways and mores? What unifies it? They do not preach a standardized, codified message. Rather, they constantly tailor that message so that it might be heard and then lived, not by generic, interchangeable people, but specific individuals at a certain place, in a certain time. Almost like Jesuit missionaries who inculturated themselves wherever they went, taking on elements of the culture while keeping the essence of Catholicism, excellent parishes are embedded in the lives of their communities, transforming them.

2. Maintain the "Edge"

Excellent parishes have something for which I can find no better word than the "edge." They constantly scrutinize themselves with even the most elementary and embarrassing of questions. If something is not working or the forecast is dim, they are willing to change. They consider how they can do what they do better, how they can better reach both those within their walls and in the larger community. These brave mariners are willing to sail stormy seas. They will not settle for mediocrity. If the salt has lost its flavor, it has no place on their table. This edge (or saltiness) of excellence brings about their vibrancy, imparts their distinctive flavor.

3. Have a "Habit of Being"

Excellent parishes have, using Flannery O'Connor's phrase about the considered life, "a habit of being." This ranges from the warm welcome of the parish secretary on an initial phone call to making sure that a first-time visitor at a liturgy isn't a stranger for long, from relevant homilies rooted in everyday experiences to religious education that is exciting and meetings that brim with expectation of what might be. Parish life is spiritually rich, God-centered, other-directed, compassionate, community enhancing and enjoyable. The great joy I witnessed on my parish visits dramatized the sheer fun that people get being in these wonderful places. They give of themselves willingly, not out of obligation or guilt. Newcomers are swept into the arms of these parishes, their needs are addressed and they are invited into meaningful parish programs and activities.

4. Are Accepting, Forgiving

It is no wonder that excellent parishes are the gateway for lapsed Catholics, for new converts, for those wearied by both life and—sometimes—other parishes. Excellent parishes are not only welcoming, but there is something in the air that says, "You are welcome here, whoever you are, whatever your circumstances might be." There are no hoops to jump through; it is easy to quickly be part of an excellent parish's life. These are warm families that welcome people to the table, no questions asked. That you are there is evidence enough that you want to be included and appreciated.

5. Are Innovative, Entrepreneurial

Excellent parishes do not hold that the Church must be completely reinvented or that gimmickry is the answer. While excellent parishes work with the resources and the rich Catholic tradition at hand, they are not restricted by them. They see new and current needs and seek to meet those needs, whether it be appealing to the often unchurched Generation Xer, educating delinquent kids, bringing a fractured community together or tapping the long-dormant desire for the authentic Spirit of God.

6. Are Willing to Take Risks

If a new beatitude could be coined, I would propose "Blessed are the risk takers." That sentiment would apply to these excellent parishes. They are not afraid of change or of new approaches. These parishes sometimes step outside their "comfort zone," whether it be in boldly asking that members tithe, that teenagers be given a real reason to come to church, that evangelization be not just for fundamentalist Christians, that a neighborhood be transformed by a parish with enough will and gumption. They look and they act beyond what is done or expected. They push the envelope gently, discreetly, wisely.

7. Are Willing to Make Mistakes

Excellent parishes do not fear failure. They realize that innovation, stepping outside accepted ways, might have its costs. But, they reason, without innovation, without walking where others have not yet walked, they will continue to trudge on in familiar, rutted pathways that may no longer lead where they want to go. They may not exactly consider themselves "fools for Christ," but they are not averse to trying new ways and admitting they did not work. If unsuccessful in some of their efforts, they go on, chastened by their experience but undaunted in their desire to serve their people and find their God.

INSTITUTIONAL LIFE

8. Rules Apply, but Are Applied Intelligently

Excellent parishes do not openly flaunt church or diocesan rules, but they are certainly not paint-by-the-numbers types or rules keepers who believe that faith is always engendered or enriched only by meticulous obedience. While they know and appreciate that they are part of a larger, worldwide church with codes and dogmas and laws, they also realize that their unique situation within their community requires them to apply church rules intelligently. They are not rebels; they practice a certain informed pragmatism.

9. Ideology and Church Battles Have Little Place

Excellent parishes are not run by ideologues who must have everyone in the pews agree with their views on current hot-button issues (celibacy, women's ordination and homosexuality among them) within the Church today. It is not that they are disloyal to the Church and do not make their views known; they just do not use such views as so many litmus tests to be passed or hurdles to be jumped. "Unless you believe this, you need not proceed any further in this parish" is not their way. The pastors and staffs of excellent parishes understand that intramural church battles neither win converts (either *to* Catholicism, or more likely, *within* Catholicism) nor promote more active participation.

10. A Different Kind of Authority Is Present

The authority of excellent parishes—both staff and leadership—derives from reflective, sensible practice, not from arbitrarily wielding some sort of ecclesial club. Excellent parishes are operated with the realization that most people will never have dealings with the Vatican or with a chancery office; people will form their opinion of what the Catholic Church stands for within the local parish. And so, the exercise of authority in these places is attractive and attracting. People want to follow because this kind of leadership anchors itself in both religious idealism and common sense. While they certainly evoke a higher power, theirs is not a controlling, regulating God, but an inviting, encouraging God. They honor people's free will and do not try to beat them into submission. They simply show and live a way that has an unassailable integrity.

Instead of protecting the faith, they present the faith—and do so in an appealing, useful way.

11. Have a Long-Term pastor

It takes a few years to know a parish and its people and to find a vision that suits a certain group of people in a certain place. Excellent parishes almost always have a pastor who has been in place for a good number of years, a person who has been able to create the atmosphere for excellence. Trust and understanding don't come overnight, even when priests and lay members use those words. Only through the crucible of daily parish life do pastors, staff and congregation begin to realize they are indeed on a common pilgrimage, that they can make mistakes, that their quest for excellence is a noble pursuit that will not be abated.

COMMUNITY

12. Based around an Idea, a Relationship

Excellent parishes serve the needs of their members well. And their members feel a special relationship, often one they may never have experienced before in their life. One convert told me he did not join *the* Catholic Church, he joined *this* Catholic Church, referring to his parish. While this may at first appear to undercut the universality of the Catholic Church, it testifies to the reality that the parish *is* the Church for most people. We do not live any longer in a one-size-fits-all world or Church. While there will always be a number of people who will go to the nearest parish—regardless of its vitality or morbidity—far more people want a fulfilling, enduring relationship.

13. Forms the Core of Their Lives

An excellent parish stands at the center of the lives of its parishioners; it becomes their base of operations. Here they find strength; here they are reinforced by the actions of others, encouraged by leadership that stands with them. In turn, they want to spread the Word wherever they are—and word about this great place they have found. Excellent parishioners are vibrant, proactive people of God, not merely anonymous members of an organization. They are universal beings, citizens of the world. Their parish moves beyond streets on a map; it travels with them wherever they go. Because they feel this way, the world becomes their mission field.

14. Many Communities within the Community

Excellent parishes realize that, while a common bond brings their people together, many communities or areas of interest exist within the parish. They do not try to homogenize such groups, but rather acknowledge and encourage their many approaches to life and God. Small faith communities provide just one way excellent parishes break down the anonymity of a large church to address the needs of people. The excellent parish sees itself as a broad tent under which many groups can gather, some of which may actually have little in common with the others.

THE WORK

15. Enough for All

Excellent parishes do not *allow* laypeople to do what was once the province of ordained clergy and vowed religious, they *encourage*—and expect—laypeople to go beyond usual, assigned tasks, often doing things that may never have been done before. Priests honestly see lay women and men as equals, and laypeople not only seek to exercise their rights but accept new responsibilities. The issue becomes one of acknowledging individual talents, seeing who can best do the job. There is no bemoaning the shrinking number of priests in excellent parishes; the work is naturally apportioned among lay and ordained. Once these "people of God" (as Vatican II pronounces all believers and seekers) are freed to express themselves, a veritable explosion of talent occurs. Every parish in this book gives testimony to that.

16. Believe in Quality

While simplicity and poverty remain exemplary Catholic virtues, excellent parishes have come to understand that such excellence has its costs. Excellent parishes pay competitive salaries to get top-notch staff. They willingly spend money for first-class educational materials. They do not simply fill a slot with the first volunteer who comes along. If that person does not measure up to the standards these parishes have set for themselves, they continue the search. While the Church has for decades relied on free, volunteer help, excellent parishes are careful how they employ volunteers so that a person's desires don't overshadow the reality of their gifts or area of competence.

SPIRITUALITY

17. Spirituality at Their Center

Excellent parishes customarily are beehives of activities; it is not extraordinary for even small churches to have thirty or forty activities and missions, and for the larger parishes to have more than a hundred. But undergirding all this is an accent on spirituality, not religion or religious belief, but spirituality. Excellent parishes consciously nurture spirituality. Prayer stands at the core not only of their liturgies, but their meetings and youth or recovery groups. Prayer provides the pathway to guidance and to God, and leads to the realization that without prayer and a deep spirituality even the best programs and plans lack a crucial component.

18. Offer an Ascent to God

Excellent parishes haven't forgotten their reason for being. They are not franchises, not outposts of an empire. They provide, first and foremost, places where people come to be close to God and to be with

others who have values that they either share or want
to acquire. These parishes preach, live, broadcast the
news that God is active in human lives at this very
moment, a hand constantly extended. These parishes
offer many ways to nurture a relationship with God,
be it in adoration of the blessed sacrament, feeding the
hungry, teaching religious education, tutoring a child
or gathering a few hundred thousand neighbors for a
street fair.

Points of
Excellence Index

*(New points of excellence lead each section, followed by an
index to points of excellence that were either noted in a sidebar or within the text.)*

1. WORSHIP

CHURCH RESTORATION AS CHURCH RENEWAL

With hundreds of once beautiful, but now aging,
Catholic churches in need of significant repair, the
question is often asked: Is a big renovation worth
it? At Our Lady Help of Christians, the answer is a
resounding "yes." But the pastor, Father Walter
Cuenin, did not subscribe to a frontal attack to make
this happen. "Too many renovation campaigns center

around history or what once was. We addressed it as a current and pressing need. We created the absolute best liturgies we could in the old space, and people began to see the problem was more than water damage and peeling paint. This was a church built in another time for a different kind of Catholic Church. But when the liturgy revs up people and they see the space doesn't work anymore and that you can't have a Vatican II life in a Vatican I building, they are ready to do something about it. Our wonderful choir was up in a loft where no one could see them; people couldn't even easily get to the front for Eucharist; we were using a plastic tub for baptism. How could you have an intimate prayer or penance service in such a cavernous place? All we were doing were things allowed by the church, nothing out of ordinary, but it became clearer and clearer that we had to redo the church. People were happy to give—some for nostalgia, but more for current needs. We raised two million dollars and the people have a great pride of ownership; for some it really changed their life. This is their spiritual home and it looks wonderful and it works for their needs."

Our Lady Help of Christians, Newton, MA

ADAPT TO LOCAL CULTURE—AND LANGUAGE

After he'd been told there "weren't very many Hispanics" in the Conway, South Carolina, community near Myrtle Beach, Father Rick LaBrecque was surprised when eighty folks showed up at his first

Spanish-language Mass several years ago. Offered as a one-time experiment, the Mass continued by popular demand and is now held each week, both at his St. James parish in Conway and at a nearby mission church in Loris. Father LaBrecque scheduled the St. James Spanish Mass at 9:15 A.M. on Sundays "to accommodate the work schedules of many of the Hispanics. Many must be at work by late morning in local restaurants," he says. This timing also allows for mingling between the Hispanic and Anglo parishioners as the latter group arrive for the next Mass. "They get a chance to mix at the coffee-and-donut table," says Father LaBrecque. Today all the office staff is bilingual. Not only does the parish offer English-as-a-second-language programs, but also Spanish-as-a-second-language programs. Two sisters from Mexico recently spent a year training laypeople to work for the Hispanic community's needs. Health Link was formed to provide translators at the local hospital for Hispanics who need health care. Other South Carolina parishes without Hispanic members send financial support for this vital work at the small but fast-growing parish of about seven hundred families.

St. James
1071 Academy Dr.
Conway, SC 29526
843-347-5168
members.aol.com/stjamessc

SIDEBARS:

IN TEXT:

2. EDUCATION

Parochial School for At-Risk Kids

"You can sit around and talk about the problems of at-risk kids, talk about how a great school would really make a difference in their lives—or, you can just go out and start one," says Father Michael Jacques. "We didn't have a building, we didn't have books, teachers or students when we said 'We're going to do this.'"

Father Jacques had read of Nativity School in New York, whose successful students were all considered "at risk," and decided that was exactly what his inner-city parish needed. He helped form a board of black New Orleans educators and was eventually given a recently closed school to use. Another school closed and contributed its library; furniture came from another. Catholic college graduates volunteered to teach just for a living stipend. "But until it's in place, how can people come forward?" Give in to your dreams; the details will take care of themselves—all with some good planning and a lot of praying.

St. Peter Claver, New Orleans

PARISH AS SEMINARY OF THE FUTURE

With declining numbers of men going into the ordained priesthood and an increasing number of lay women and men eager to participate more fully in church life, Father Patrick Brennan sees the parish fulfilling many of the teaching functions once reserved to seminaries. "We always encourage people to go off for training or courses or workshops, but at Holy Family we've found that we can just as effectively bring great teachers to the parish and have many more people participate. Some of our people have undertaken the two-year leadership at Loyola University but we have also brought training close to where people live. Chicago Theological Union offers courses here; Dominican University is working on offering a B.A. in pastoral ministry. There are tremendous resources not more than minutes away from every parish; we just have to find them and make them both attractive and readily available to people who, while they have busy lives, are hungry for this."

Holy Family, Inverness, IL

A CENTER FOR LAY MINISTRY

Because they believe that the future of the Church is in lay ministry, parishioners at Pax Christi in Eden Prairie, Minnesota, have done something about it. They founded the Leaven Center for the development of lay ministry, which offers accredited as well as continuing education courses through cooperation with a nearby college. In courses as diverse as "Leading Change in the Congregation" to "Evenings of Prayer with the Mystics," students from all professional, educational and religious backgrounds have the chance to learn new leadership skills as well as study different expressions of spirituality. This is not just a program for would-be theological students; it also reaches out to those at varying places on the spiritual journey. Ecumenical yet thoroughly infused with the spirit of Vatican II, the Leaven Center has attracted advisors and support from diverse individuals of different faiths.

A new project at the Leaven Center will establish a Catholic Leadership Network, not unlike the already well-known Protestant Leadership Network in Dallas,

Texas. This ambitious effort will bring some of the brightest stars in parish life together to exchange ideas and practical solutions to everyday "in the trenches" problems faced by parish leaders across the country.

The Leaven Center
12100 Pioneer Trail
Eden Prairie, MN 55347
612-946-9709
www.leavencenter.org/whopax.html

TRAINING MINISTERS FROM WITHIN—AND PAYING FOR IT

When Father Douglas Doussan wanted to take the lay leaders of his New Orleans parish to the next level by offering them advanced education, eleven parishioners, aged thirty to fifty-seven, jumped at the chance. He offered to pay half their tuition for a master's program in pastoral studies at the respected Loyola University. In exchange, the students agreed to give back eight to ten hours a week for five years in ministry work at the parish. "Most of those who joined the program were already leaders in parish life," says pastoral associate Sister Kathleen Pittman. "But this was a chance and a challenge they welcomed." Six of the original eleven parishioners enrolled in the master's program have already graduated and are working in ministries in the parish—doing everything from directing religious education to serving in the Family Life program, from improving liturgy to advancing youth programs. "The good this has done for our parish is hard to measure. Those who participated formed tight bonds with one another, which gives us the bonus of great staff relations. Parishioners like knowing that they helped do this—helped support the training of their own leaders."

St. Gabriel the Archangel
4700 Pineda St.
New Orleans, LA 70126-3599
504-282-0296
www.stgabe.net

SIDEBARS:
Training lay leaders—creating a lay institute—St. Pius X, p. 22
Family-conscious ministry—Holy Family, p. 62
Pastor as missionary—St. Peter Claver, p. 77
Catholic education—and free—St. Francis of Assisi, Wichita,
    p. 121

IN TEXT:
Concentration on youth—Our Lady Help of Christians, p. 15
Generation X—St. Pius X, p. 23
Life Teen—St. Pius X, pp. 27, 33
Adult education—Holy Family, p. 63
A priest is "educated"—St. Peter Claver, p. 78
Excellent parish schools—St. Pius X, p. 35
    —St. Peter Claver, p. 82
Sensible religious education—St. Francis of Assisi, Wichita,
    p. 124

3. EVANGELIZATION

Music: A Tool of Evangelization

The African American St. Augustine Catholic Church choir in Memphis takes sacred music and makes the most of it as a means of evangelization. "We try to present music that is spiritually uplifting, infusing new, fresh life into it by using popular styles to enhance the sermon or the readings of the day," says choir director Albert Langston. "We use many types—classical, traditional hymns, contemporary—but our biggest emphasis is on gospel music." The ultimate purpose of the choir is to praise the Lord through song. In doing this, the choir works to assist the congregation in a more active participation in Mass, the parish and their faith. Beyond the church walls, the choir can be seen at events around the city and in other states, spreading the evangelization of their music to thousands of people at concerts, dedications, celebrations or memorial services. For many, it's eye-opening to see African American Catholics praising God through song.

To keep up with their active schedule, the choir benefits from a dedicated support group. "These are parishioners that love us so much that they travel with us, help us with our fund raisers—the fish fry, the Mardi Gras dance—act as ushers at events and much more," says Langston. "They sometimes rent a second bus for themselves when we travel, then sell seats on their bus to pay for the choir members' bus fares. Their help is invaluable."

St. Augustine
1169 Kerr Ave.
Memphis, TN 38106
901-774-2297
www.cdom.org/parishes/st%20augustine

REACHING OUT TO GENERATION X

A downtown Minneapolis church accessible via sky-way, St. Olaf's reaches out to Generation X. Their half-hour cable access show, *Generation Cross*, tells Xers they don't have to accept the label that says they don't stand for anything. The show is "a lighthearted, entertaining look at what it means to be Catholic," says parish administrator Carol Bishop. Begun as an offshoot of the televised weekly liturgy, regular features cover questions and answers on the Church, interviews, visits to Rome, even recipes. A huge success in the Minneapolis area, the show is now also seen in Boston and may soon go national. "This is religious television like you've never seen it before," says St. Olaf staff member Mark Croteau. "It's a fast-paced show that manages to catechize and entertain simultaneously. But like any program we do, we hope it reflects our mission to serve as a 'living sign of Christ's saving presence in the heart of the city.'" The response to *Generation Cross* shows the impact on young adults—the show receives hundreds of e-mails each month.

St. Olaf's
215 So. 8th St.
Minneapolis, MN 55402
612-332-7471
www.saintolaf.org

ANNUAL MEGA BLOCK PARTY

A block party may seem an unusual way to grow a church. But at Old St. Pat's in Chicago's West Loop, this annual tradition—started in 1984 when the parish had four members—has helped increase registered families to over 3,500 today. The block party was conceived by then new pastor Father Jack Wall as a way to reestablish a feeling of community in the seedy, run-down area that surrounded Chicago's oldest parish. The church has blossomed as the block party has grown to attract a million people during the third weekend in July. Billed as the "World's Largest Block Party," nationally and internationally known rock, jazz and swing bands are featured, and the best vendors from all over the city provide food. "Old St. Pat's is a mission-driven church rather than a parish of geo graphic boundaries," says Bridget Boland, parish communications director. "The block party is one more way we can extend a warm invitation to people to 'come join our church!'" Volunteers are key to keeping this annual party alive; fourteen hundred of them help each year. The block party has become popular with young adults as a place to meet people—over sixty "block party couples" who met at the event were later married.

Old St. Pat's
718 W. Adams St.
Chicago, IL 60661
312-648-1021
www.oldstpats.org

SIDEBAR:

Evangelizing: steps to greater lay involvement—St. Pius X, p. 31
Ministry of presence—Catholic Area Parishes, p. 53
Communications ministry: beyond the walls Holy Family, p. 64
Welcoming committee visits— St. Mark's, p. 133

IN TEXT:

Ecumenical welcome—Our Lady Help of Christians, p. 9
Conversion within Catholicism—Catholic Area Parishes, p. 49
Discovering needs people don't know they have—Holy Family, p. 65
"Evangelical" Catholic Church—Holy Family, p. 69
Warm welcome: gateway back for lapsed Catholics—St. Francis of Assisi, Portland, p. 99
Hospitality—St. Francis of Assisi, Wichita, p. 120
Stewardship spreads to diocese—St. Francis of Assisi, Wichita, p. 126
Taking Catholicism into world—St. Mark's, p. 140

4. OUTREACH

LETTING MINISTRIES EMERGE

The concern was common enough: Martha Armendariz's mother, Cecilia, was growing older and had no outlet for her creativity and no safe place to gather with her friends. Martha, knowing that St. Pius X was the kind of parish open to innovation, began to ask her mother and other senior citizens what kind of classes they would enjoy. Then, matching their interests with teachers in the parish, she began to slowly construct what eventually became the St. Cecilia Personal

Enrichment Ministry. In eight-week segments, meeting for an hour or two, parishioners are invited to classes in photography, sign language, painting, arts and crafts, floral arrangement, guitar, folklorico dancing, self-defense, rosary making and home maintenance. "The pastor need not be involved," says Martha, embodying the St. Pius X spirit, "everyone pitched in and it has been a great success and a great community builder among those that might not have this kind of opportunity to get out, have fun and be productive."

St. Pius X, El Paso, TX

GREEN SPACE——FAITH AS ECOLOGY

The St. Francis Park, which sits behind the church and takes up nearly a city block, is a testing ground of sorts to see if a predominantly middle-class congregation can share the space with the homeless. "It is very Franciscan to be sure," says Valerie Chapman, the pastoral administrator, "and it is symbolic of respect for the environment and a celebration of creation. But, because it is not some neat, walled-off enclave, but open to all classes of people, it is a statement that as we treasure the things of nature, we cannot hoard them, they are for everyone to share and enjoy. Yes, there may be litter there, yes, and having a Port-a-Potty may not be considered the most pristine touch, but how better to show hospitality than with a quiet, green——but gated——place to sit?"

St. Francis of Assisi, Portland, OR

5. SPIRITUALITY/INREACH

WARMTH ATTRACTS

At St. Pius X, the prevailing attitude is that people coming to church have had a tough week and that there should be an *embracero*—preferably actual, but surely conveyed—for everyone who walks through the front doors. "We try to get it across with our greeters and with each parishioner that how we welcome people is so very important," says Father Arturo

Banuelas. "I'm not talking about false happiness, either, but a deep love that must be felt. Warmth is attractive; it is contagious. It is what we hear over and over again from people who come to us. 'I never felt so welcome in a Catholic church before,' they often say. We all want to be warmly welcomed, to feel we belong, we are accepted. That is our first job, before we ever go into the church to begin the liturgy."

St. Pius X, El Paso, TX

SMALL CHRISTIAN COMMUNITIES: KEY TO RURAL
AND SMALL-TOWN MINISTRY

When Sister Clara Stang came to the five-parish cluster in rural Minnesota, no small Christian communities existed. "People out here would say that they know each other so well already, why would they need something like that?" says Sister Clara. But she knew that while everyone did know everyone else in town, they really didn't know what was going on inside one another. She wanted to create a way that they could openly and in confidence share their lives and their faith. She attended a diocesan workshop given by Father Art Baronowski, an expert on small Christian communities. And then she trained fifteen people, using one of Father Baronowski's books, to be leaders. Although there was initial resistance to joining these groups, each week Sister Clara and the cluster staff would draw up a series of questions suggested by the week's scriptural readings that could be used in the small groups. "We avoided anything churchy," she says. "We stayed practical. The questions were always about how the scripture can be applied to real life." Gradually people became more comfortable with the small community concept and today some two hundred members of the parishes meet in nineteen groups. Next-door neighbors really got to know each other. "I think it helps people to see that it's not just God and me alone in this life, but we are together as a parish. We have support from one another. We're all struggling; we all need to realize that."

Catholic Area Parishes—Benson, DeGraff, Danvers, Clontarf and Murdock, MN

FAITH & WORK BREAKFASTS

Another notable ministry at St. Olaf's in Minneapolis is their six-year-old Faith & Work Breakfast Series. In conjunction with the University of St. Thomas, it's a monthly, seasonal effort in which business leaders address topics "relative to living out our faith in and through our work. The program examines issues of values, justice and integrity," says Carol Bishop, parish administrator. Starting at 7 A.M., participants have breakfast and hear speakers on topics such as "Corporate Responsibility and Human Rights in a World Community" or "Faith, Values and Public Service in a Pluralistic Society." The talk and discussion end promptly at 8:15 so business people can fit the series into their schedules. As the series brochure notes, "Faith & Work is counter-cultural; it is about bringing our faith and spirituality to all dimensions of our lives."

St. Olaf's
215 So. 8th St.
Minneapolis, MN 55402
612-332-7471
www.saintolaf.org

REPAIRING PAST DAMAGE: PASTOR APOLOGIZES
FOR CHURCH WRONGS

At St. Catherine of Siena in Rialto, California, the popular "Renewal Weekends" have a special emphasis on healing from pain inflicted by the Church. During the "Barriers" section of the retreat, Pastor Father Howard Lincoln *apologizes* for any past hurt imposed by a priest or nun serving as a representative of the Church. "He apologizes for a wide range of things — for not getting to the hospital in time to give last rites to a loved one, for divorced people who've had trouble getting an annulment, for making it difficult for parents to have a baby baptized, for a homily that may have offended someone," says pastoral associate Kay Halder.

One couple on a recent retreat had moved to another parish because of a conflict they'd had with the parish school seven years earlier, prior to Father Lincoln's becoming pastor. They were at the retreat under duress; they were required to attend to get sacramental preparation for one of their children, yet something in Father Lincoln's talk touched upon the hurt they'd felt years ago. They were deeply moved and, finally, healed. "There are so many stories of people who've been changed by the retreat," said Kay.

St. Catherine's learned about Renewal Weekends from a church in San Diego, but adapted it to the needs of the parish. They offer the retreats in Spanish and English, emphasizing lay leadership and lay speakers. Members of parishes from as far away as North Carolina attend the weekends to carry inspiration back to their home churches.

St. Catherine of Siena
339 N. Sycamore Ave.
Rialto, CA 92376-3517
909-875-1360
www.stcatherine.net

MAKING THE MOST OF THE BULLETIN

Nearly every Catholic church produces a bulletin. But at Old St. Pat's, the bulletin is so chock full of useful information, it's hard for parishioners to throw it out. Maybe that's the idea. Granted, not all parishes can have the sweeping range of activities, volunteer opportunities, programs, missions and services that Old St. Pat's does, but almost any parish could find a feature in this bulletin that might work in their own. For instance, there is a "What Can We Do for You?" box with ample blank space for comments and suggestions that can then be placed in the collection basket. The bulletin also includes a registration form for new members or current members who need to update their information. There's also a place for nonmembers to indicate that they wish to be considered "associates" (they regularly attend events, programs or Masses) or "friends" (they lend occasional support as event attendees, volunteers or as financial contributors). Old St. Pat's recognizes and encourages the fact that while not everyone may choose to be a member, there are many ways individuals can support the parish—and the bulletin may be the only way to establish contact with these people. Above all, the bulletin is cleanly designed, easy to read and *looks* interesting. That's due to the work of an editorial board and a graphic designer, but with the proliferation of quality desktop publishing software, a more compelling, reader-friendly bulletin is within the reach of most parishes.

Old St. Pat's
718 W. Adams St.
Chicago, IL 60661
312-648-1021
www.oldstpats.org

SUNDAY SUPPERS

One of the difficulties faced by growing parishes is keeping alive a feeling of intimacy among its parishioners. Retreats or small communities help, but so can something as simple as a Sunday supper. Once a month at Old St. Pat's, members and others are invited to a buffet dinner in the church hall. Beginning at 5:45 with welcome and refreshments, the supper costs $10. A speaker is provided; recently it was Paulette Mulligan, R.N., M.S., whose after-dinner talk was "Unleash Your Creativity." Followed by coffee and dessert, the half-hour presentations are brief—in fact the supper is over by 8 P.M. "It's a way for people to gather, see many of the same faces and some new ones, have a meal and hear someone speak on an inspirational or spiritual topic," says Bridget Borland, parish communications director. "It's another way to connect with the church and with one another."

Old St. Pat's
718 W. Adams St.
Chicago, IL 60625
312-648-1021
www.oldstpats.org

SIDEBAR:

IN TEXT:

6. ORGANIZATION

No Paid Lay Ministry Staff

The dreams at St. Pius X are great, but the parish budget is not. So, while there are thirty-nine ministries, there is no paid lay ministry staff. "We don't ask enough of people; we are often too shy to ask that they give themselves away—which is exactly what people want to do," says Father Arturo Banuelas. "But their work must be real, not just busy work. It must be honored, genuine, respected, supported. Here at St. Pius X, lay women and men are not doing volunteer work; they are involved in ministries. They are ministers. We have to stop being 'the Church' and let the people take over."

St. Pius X, El Paso, TX

LEARNING FROM PROTESTANT MEGACHURCHES

Father Patrick Brennan admits something that might be on the mind of many a priest and bishop, but is rarely spoken publicly: his benchmark of excellence is a Protestant megachurch. "We differ on theology with Willowcreek, but not at all with their excellence in everything they do. Education, evangelization, communication are all first-rate." Holy Family is in the same general area as Willowcreek, one of the biggest and most successful of the megachurches that have come into prominence in recent years. "Willowcreek showed us about marketing, about presenting what we have so that it is looked upon as desirable, needed. You don't have to subscribe to everything these churches do, but if you look closer at them, they can teach us so much."

Holy Family, Inverness, IL

PRIEST SHORTAGE? ANSWER: LAY INVOLVEMENT

With 1,000 people involved in 122 ministries, Holy Family is a stunning example of lay involvement. "We put a special emphasis on lay ministry each year at Easter and the weeks leading up to Pentecost," says Father Patrick Brennan. "We talk of a personal resurrection to the Word; we talk of a call to mission for everyone at Pentecost and then lead into a 'gifted' course so that people might discern God's call. We make it clear that we are not trying to necessarily funnel them into work in the parish. God's call for them might be outside the Church. And when we look for leaders among them, and for filling staff positions, we look for what I would call 'seminal goodness and giftedness,' together with an openness to training and ongoing formation. We are not looking for nouveau clerics, but rather people who want to do their ministry *with* people, not *for* people. We look for servant-leaders, not autocrats. You can tell pretty quickly what a person's motivations and level of openness are. Just don't try to jam the next available person into the job that seems to need being done right then "

Holy Family, Inverness, IL

SATELLITE CHURCHES

When Father Jose Menendez was named pastor of Corpus Christi parish in Miami several years ago, he sent church teams to call at the homes of all the people within the parish boundaries. He found a diverse group of mostly poor Hispanic people. They were from Puerto Rico, the Dominican Republic, Colombia, Peru, Cuba and other Latin countries. Many were unable to attend Mass because they lacked transportation.

Father Menendez's solution was to empower laypeople from several areas to set up storefront missions for each of the larger groups, four in all. At first, the people met at their respective missions on Wednesday nights, gradually building a feeling of community through their weekly gatherings. Now Mass is held at these four different locations each week in addition to the main church. "The missions are vibrant, with committed leaders, parishioners willing to work hard and a true community spirit," says Father Menendez. Base communities have flourished out of the missions, enriching evangelization efforts. In Miami as in other cities, many Protestant churches had been drawing Hispanics with the storefront approach—by taking their church to the people. The missions of Corpus Christi allow Hispanic Catholics the option of attending the Church in which many of them were born.

Another important aspect of the missions is that laypeople have learned to consider the missions "theirs." The people truly "own" the missions. They make the effort to find the best materials they can to furnish the missions—the altar might come from an Argentine Lutheran church, the pews from a church being torn down in Georgia. "All the missions are very different and very beautiful—giving these people who've never had anything something to be proud of," says Father Menendez. "It gives them hope that they can achieve more in life. They *need* to have hope."

Corpus Christi
3220 NW 7th Ave.
Miami, FL 33127
305-635-1331

TITHING IN THE INNER CITY

A poor, inner-city parish with mostly immigrant members may seem an unusual place to preach tithing, but Father Jose Menendez does. "They give their time, they give their talent and they share their treasure; when I came here twelve years ago, the parish had a thousand people and the collection was between $900 and $1,000 a week. Now we have seventeen hundred and our collection is about $6,000 a week." The feeling of parish ownership developed among the members has a natural extension in tithing.

Corpus Christi
3220 NW 7th Ave.
Miami, FL 33127
305-635-2031

SIDEBAR:

A staff with common vision, yet willing to dissent—Our Lady
    Help of Christians, p. 18
Cluster ministries—Catholic Area Parishes, p. 46
Lay pastor advantages—St. Francis, Portland, p. 96
Stewardship—time and talent first—St. Francis, Wichita, p. 112

IN TEXT:

Hire excellent lay staff—Our Lady Help of Christians, p. 5
Sensible personnel policies—Our Lady Help of Christians, p. 14
Rectory a home, not an office—Our Lady Help of Christians,
    p. 14
New Hispanic ministries—St. Pius X, pp. 20, 23
Priest shortage?—St. Pius X, p. 30

Index of Excellent Parishes

Here are the excellent parishes the Parish/Congregation Study has found throughout America. Of course, there are other excellent parishes we have not found, but these, we feel, are representative of what is best in local church life today. Most entries have a short note about that parish's emphases and programs.

ALABAMA
Auburn

St. Michael
302 East Magnolia Ave.   334-887-5540
Auburn, AL 36830   www.auburn.edu/~stmcso1/

Associated with Auburn University; Pan y Vino retreats; out-reach programs.

Daphne

Christ the King
PO Box 549   334-626-2343
Daphne, AL 36526   www.ctheking.org

Addresses needs of fast-growing area; has a Blue Army ministry (First Saturday devotions); the home visitation and respite ministry visits sick and gives caregivers a break.

Dothan

St. Columba
2700 West Main St.   334-793-5802
Dothan, AL 36301   rcamobile.org/dothanco.html

Family Life Ministry; Life Teen; Iona Group ministers to and with seniors; weekly Spanish Mass and monthly Vietnamese Mass.

Mobile

St. Ignatius
3704 Springhill Ave.   334-342-9221
Mobile, AL 36608   rcamobile.org/mobsigna.html

Stephen ministry trains volunteers to help people in need; strong youth and young adult programs with full-time minister; blue ribbon school.

Mobile

Corpus Christi
6300 McKenna Dr.
Mobile, AL 36608   334-342-1852

Hospitable suburban church has award-winning school, many young families and copastors who innovate; singles ministry.

Mobile
ST. DOMINIC
4156 Burma Rd.   334-661-5130
Mobile, AL 36693   www.stdominicparish.org

Suburban parish with a K–8 school that runs learning disability program; pastoral care to homebound; comprehensive and flexible RCIA.

Mobile
MOST PURE HEART OF MARY
304 Sengstak St.   334-432-3344
Mobile, AL 36601   www.josephite.com/parish/al/phm

Inner-city African American parish with school; outstanding leaders.

Montgomery
ST. BEDE
3870 Atlanta Hwy.
Montgomery, AL 36109
334-272-3463   www.stbede.org

Life Teen and Catholic Heart Work Camp for youth; strong music programs; social justice work includes pro-life, AIDS outreach and direct aid to poor.

Wetumpka
ST. MARK
Hwy. 170
PO Box 765
Wetumpka, AL 36092   334-285-7000

Small, but fast-growing parish where hospitality is stressed.

ALASKA
Anchorage
OUR LADY OF GUADALUPE
3900 Wisconsin St.
Anchorage, AK 99517   907-248-2000

Diverse, growing community; high degree of lay involvement; active Hispanic community.

Skagway
ST. THERESE
Box 496
Skagway, AK 99840   907-983-2271

Small mission church is run by woman administrator; priest visits once a month.

ARIZONA
Mesa
ST. TIMOTHY
1730 W. Guadalupe   602-775-5200
Mesa, AZ 85202   www.sttims-mesa.org

One hundred active lay ministries; originated national Life Teen program and now trains other parishes; strong music ministry; Paz de Cristo Center serves meals to homeless; nursery and preschool.

Mesa
CHRIST THE KING
1551 E. Dana Ave.
Mesa, AZ 85204   602-964-1719

Christ Renews His Parish retreats revitalize parishioners and create leaders; strong Life Teen program; ministry of stewardship in its sixth year.

Peoria
ST. CHARLES BORROMEO
8615 W. Peoria Ave.
Peoria, AZ 85380   623-979-3418

Phoenix

ST. CATHERINE OF SIENA
6200 S. Central Ave.
Phoenix, AZ 85040   602-276-5581

Masses offered in Spanish and English.

Scottsdale

ST. PATRICK
10815 N. 84th St.
Scottsdale, AZ 85260   480-998-3843

Tucson

OUR MOTHER OF SORROWS
1800 S. Kolb Rd.   520-888-1530
Tucson, AZ 85705   www.omosparish.org

Retreat ministry offers several retreats each year; Alienated
Catholics Anonymous helps Catholics rediscover their faith
through a six-week program; several charity and justice service ministries.

ARKANSAS
Little Rock

OUR LADY OF GOOD COUNSEL
1321 S. Van Buren St.
Little Rock, AR 72204   501-666-5073

Welcoming church with lively music and liturgies; perpetual
adoration; Life Teen; single parent group; paid family life
director; school.

CALIFORNIA
Chino

OUR LADY OF GUADALUPE
5048 D St.
Chino, CA 91710   909-591-9402
                        www.sbdiocese.org/parishes/chino.htm#olg

Strong Life Teen program; weekly prayer group; *Jovenes para
Christo* (a young adult group) meets for outreach and social
activities.

Los Angeles
NATIVITY
953 W. 57th St.
Los Angeles, CA 90037   323-759-1562

Urban, bilingual cluster parish with liturgy preparation team; bilingual pastoral council; popular parish fiestas.

Los Angeles
ST. AGATHA
2610 S. Mansfield Ave.
Los Angeles, CA 90016   323-935-8127

Strong on community outreach; Sunday gospel Mass.

Los Angeles
ST. BRIDGET
510 Cottage Home St.   323-222-5518
Los Angeles, CA 90012   www.unique.net/stbridget/

Masses in Cantonese and English; strong choir; community center; youth activities.

Moraga
ST. MONICA
1001 Camino Pablo   925-376-6900
Moraga, CA 94556   www.stmonicamoraga.com/

Suburban parish; good outreach to children and seniors; high lay involvement; enthusiastic pastoral council.

Oakland
ST. MARY-ST. FRANCIS
634 21st St.   510-832-5057
Oakland, CA 94607   www.sm-sfds.org

Trilingual parish with twelve ethnic groups; quality liturgy, preaching and music; tutoring programs in local schools; four-month winter shelter; volunteers for GED program; days of prayer and reflection.

Pleasant Hill

CHRIST THE KING
199 Brandon Rd.   925-682-2486
Pleasant Hill, CA 94523   www.ctkph.org

Strong, enthusiastic liturgies and homilies; Lifeworks program for families with young children; social justice consciousness; many creative programs.

Pleasanton

ST. AUGUSTINE
3999 Bernal Ave.   510-846-4489
Pleasanton, CA 94566   www.st-augustine-plsntn.org

Stewardship parish is developing small faith communities; hospitable returning Catholics program.

Pomona

SACRED HEART
1215 S. Hamilton Blvd.
Pomona, CA 91766   909-622-4553

Rialto

ST. CATHERINE OF SIENA
339 N. Sycamore Ave.   909-875-1360
Rialto, CA 92376-3517   www.stcatherine.net

Monthly renewal weekends bring about healing and strengthen faith; SCYN youth night is held twice monthly with Mass and program in hall; bilingual religious education for children and parents.

San Diego

CHRIST THE KING
29 North 32nd St.
San Diego, CA 92102   619-231-8906

Welcoming, multicultural community; known for choirs; good outreach; facilitates three cultures working together.

San Francisco

ST. TERESA OF AVILA
390 Missouri St.   415-285-5272
San Francisco, CA 94107   www.st-teresas.org

Small Christian communities; liturgy committee plans twenty special liturgies each year; works ecumenically on housing and immigration issues.

San Gabriel

ST. ANTHONY
1901 S. San Gabriel Blvd.   626-288-8912
San Gabriel, CA 91776   members.aol.com/sttonysg

Strong evangelization team; religious education program draws hundreds of children; multicultural congregation.

San Jose

MOST HOLY TRINITY
2040 Nassau Dr.
San Jose, CA 95122-1795   408-729-0101

Hospitable; multicultural; offers Masses in five languages; professional liturgist and presiders; contracted musicians; faith-sharing groups; emphasis on unity.

Santa Ana

ST. JOSEPH
727 Minter St.
Santa Ana, CA 92701   714-542-4411

Multicultural with Masses in English and Spanish; bilingual initiation process and sacramental preparation; collaborates on projects with churches of other denominations.

Santa Monica

ST. MONICA
725 California Ave.   310-393-9287
Santa Monica, CA 90403   www.stmonica.net

Welcoming atmosphere; Young Ministering Adults; faith groups; sense of community; strong music and peace and justice ministries.

Thousand Oaks
St. Paschal Baylon
155 E. Janss Rd.   805-496-0222
Thousand Oaks, CA 91360   www.stpaschal.org

Wide variety of programs for all ages, including youth program and seniors' group; Project Response provides food for homeless.

COLORADO
Arvada
Spirit of Christ
7400 West 80th Ave.   303-422-9173
Arvada, CO 80003   www.spiritofchrist.org

Emphasizes hospitality, justice and stewardship; has sixty-five small church communities with full-time director; liturgy and music have full-time directors.

Littleton
Pax Christi
5761 McArthur Ranch Rd.
Littleton, CO 80124   303-799-1036

Young, fast-growing parish built a chapel of hay bales; founded with a lay pastor; befriender program (trained volunteers offer support to those experiencing life stresses); emphasis on stewardship; strong liturgies.

CONNECTICUT
Bridgeport
St. Peter
695 Colorado Ave.
Bridgeport, CT 06605   203-366-5611

Hartford
Immaculate Conception
574 Park St.
Hartford, CT 06106   860-525-1522

Hartford

SACRED HEART
49 Winthrop St.
Hartford, CT 06103   860-527-6459

All Masses in Spanish; special attention given to children's needs through mentoring, tutoring, athletics and more; strong social action committee addresses myriad needs of community.

New Haven

ST. THOMAS MORE CATHOLIC CENTER AND CHAPEL
268 Park St.
New Haven, CT 06511   203-777-5537
www.pantheon.cis.ya6.edu/~morehous/

Stratford

ST. JAMES
2070 Main St.
Stratford, CT 06615   203-375-5887

Welcoming parish with many support groups; lay participation encouraged.

Windham

SAGRADO CORAZON DE JESUS
61 Club Rd.
Windham, CT 06280   860-423-5131

Hispanic parish has all Masses in Spanish; strong music with three choirs; adult education with good participation in workshops; good youth activities.

DISTRICT OF COLUMBIA

SHRINE OF THE SACRED HEART
3211 Pine St. NW
Washington, DC 20010   202-234-8000
www.parishes.org/sacredheartdc.html

Mostly Spanish-speaking parish has Masses in three languages; Spanish-speaking charismatic movement develops leaders and evangelizes; catechetical program for Spanish-speaking children; strong liturgical celebrations.

OUR LADY QUEEN OF THE AMERICAS
2200 California St. NW
Washington, DC 20008-3902   202-332-8838

Nongeographic Hispanic parish provides a home away from home; services include language classes, etc. with ESL, GED and citizenship classes to more than fifteen hundred students of all ages; tutoring; employment help; Sunday cafeteria service.

HOLY TRINITY
3513 N St. NW   202-337-2840
Washington, DC 20007   www.holytrinitydc.org

Fosters lay involvement in worship; runs clothing drives; food distribution to the poor; twenty-four eucharistic celebrations weekly; RCIA; Coming Home.

ST. AUGUSTINE
1425 V St. NW   202-265-1470
Washington, DC 20009   www.parishes.org/augustine.html

Oldest predominantly African American parish in Washington, D.C.; emphasizes spiritual, social and economic development.

FLORIDA
Altamonte Springs
ST. MARY MAGDELEN
861 Maitland Ave.
Altamonte Springs, FL 32701   407-831-1212

Excellent Spanish and English liturgies; child and adult day care centers; school; religious and adult education; Catholics Coming Home (works to bring estranged Catholics back); works with Habitat for Humanity.

Boca Raton

St. Jude
21689 Toledo Rd.   561-392-8172
Boca Raton, FL 33433   www.gate.net/~stjudes

Prayer and meditation garden; senior friendship group;
masses in Spanish and English.

Brandon

Nativity
705 E. Brandon Blvd.
Brandon, FL 33511   813-681-4608
                www.nativitycatholicchurch.org/contents.htm

Strong music program includes adult chorale with a hundred
members, Hispanic choir and children's and teens' choirs.

Indialantic

Holy Name of Jesus
3050 North Hwy. A1A   321-773-2783
Indialantic, FL 32903   www.hnj.org/

Weekend retreats; small communities; perpetual adoration;
full-immersion baptismal font; supports Food for the Poor
and Habitat for Humanity; active thrift shop supports aid to
poor.

Jacksonville

Christ the King
742 Arlington Rd.   904-724-0080
Jacksonville, FL 32211   www.jacksonville.net/~ctks/

Stewardship parish that provides tuition-free school.

Miami

St. Catherine of Siena
9200 SW 107th Ave.
Miami, FL 33176   305-274-6333
                dcps.dade.k12.fl.us/palmetto-ad/st_cathr.htm

Diverse Hispanic community with many nationalities; ministry to sick and homebound; two nursing homes; strong lay-

supported RCIA; thirty-eight religious education classes run by a full-time lay director of religious education; community classes; fiestas.

Miami

St. Dominic
5909 NW 7th St.
Miami, FL 33126   305-264-0181

Predominantly Hispanic parish with excellent Dominican preaching, prayerful liturgies, strong RCIA and lay formation programs and collaborative leadership; runs a successful senior day care/club with local community hospital.

Miami

St. Agatha
1111 SW 107th Ave.   305-222-1500
Miami, FL 33174   www.geocities.com/~stagatha/

Urban parish; a focus on family in religious education; base communities help evangelization and lay leadership; Masses in Spanish and English.

Miami

St. Brendan
8725 SW 32 St.
Miami, FL 33165   305-221-0881

Miami

St. Mary's Cathedral
7525 NW 2nd Ave.
Miami, FL 33150   305-759-4531

Mix of ethnic ministries including one to Haitians.

Miami

St. Louis
7270 SW 120th St.   305-238-7562
Miami, FL 33156   www.stlouiscatholic.org

Ministry to high school youth; Life in the Spirit seminars lead people to a richer faith; numerous outreach ministries, including aid to a sister diocese in Haiti.

Miami

MOTHER OF CHRIST
14141 SW 26th St.   305-559-6111
Miami, Fl. 33175   www.motherofchrist.net

Young and welcoming parish; strong stewardship ministry;
day care center; youth summer camp; strong youth ministries; starting new school for grades pre-K through eight.

Miami

CORPUS CHRISTI
3220 NW 7th Ave.
Miami, FL 33127   305-635-2031

Has four mission churches to serve diverse inner-city
groups; promotes formation of base communities; strong
sense of lay ownership.

Miami Beach

ST. PATRICK
3716 Garden Ave.   305-531-1125
Miami Beach, FL 33140   www.stpatrickchurch.org

Mixed Anglo and Hispanic parish; sense of responsibility
among members; good training of leaders.

Orange Park

ST. CATHERINE
1649 Kingsley Ave.   904-269-1511
Orange Park, FL 32073   www.stcatherinesiena.com

Suburban church with strong RCIA; program to help local
soup kitchen; has a Spanish Mass; MOMS program (spirituality for young mothers).

Tampa

ST. TIMOTHY
4015 Ragg Rd.   813-968-1077
Tampa, FL 33694-0129   www.sttimsonline.org

Numerous human concerns ministries; parish festival.

Winter Park

St. Margaret Mary
526 N. Park Ave.   407-647-3392
Winter Park, FL 32789   www.stmargaretmary.org

Participative, well-planned liturgies directed by a dedicated
team; scripture classes; lecture series; programs for seniors;
Family, Friends, & Chicken Soup program provides nonmed-
ical assistance to those in need.

GEORGIA
Alpharetta

St. Thomas Aquinas
535 Rucker Rd.   770-475-4501
Alpharetta, GA 30004   www.sta.org

Small faith communities; religious education with emphasis
on adult formation; Life Teen; outreach to recent Hispanic
immigrants.

Atlanta

Cathedral of Christ the King
2699 Peachtree Rd. NE
Atlanta, GA 30152   404-233-2145
                    www.mindspring.com/~ctk/index.html

Ministries to the homebound and hospitalized; well-attended
women's Bible study; ten choirs.

Port Wentworth

Our Lady of Lourdes
501 S. Coastal Hwy.
Port Wentworth, GA 31407   912-964-0219

Small parish founded in 1940; strong children's religious education; bereavement committee.

HAWAII
KAILUA
ST. JOHN VIANNEY
920 Keolu Dr.
Kailua, HI 96734   808-262-8317

Energetic, participatory suburban parish with 225 members helping liturgical ministries; quality liturgical music; K–8 school.

IDAHO
Boise
ST. MARK'S
7503 Northview
Boise, ID 83704   208-375-6651
www.cyberhighway.net/~stmarks/parish/stmarkshome.html

See parish profile, pp. 129–148.

ILLINOIS
Chicago
OLD ST. PAT'S
718 W. Adams St.   312-648-1021
Chicago, IL 60661   www.oldstpats.org

Inclusive and hospitable; huge yearly block party; summer suppers; Crossroads Center (faith, work and justice concerns); works for adult literacy, HIV/kids, food bank, homeless shelter and outreach to needy.

Chicago
ST. GERTRUDE
1420 Granville Ave.
Chicago, IL 60660   773-764-3621

Works with community group on health care, housing, justice; monthly meal/meeting for four to six new couples at rectory for hospitality and discussion; monthly book club.

Chicago
St. Benedict the African
340 W. 66th St.
Chicago, IL 60621   312-873-4464

Open, hospitable, urban African American parish with full-immersion baptismal pool; strong choirs; women's prayer group; men's club; scripture-sharing group.

Chicago
St. James
2942 S. Wabash Ave.
Chicago, IL 60616   312-842-1919

Dynamic 150-year-old parish; K–8 school; social care outreach to seniors and the poor in the parish neighborhood; prayerful liturgies; good music and preaching.

Chicago
St. Agnes
2651 S. Central Park Ave.
Chicago, IL 60623   773-522-0142

Largest Hispanic parish in the Midwest; strong religious education with 750 enrolled; elementary school; lay leadership encouraged.

Chicago
St. Sylvester
2157 N. Humboldt Blvd.
Chicago, IL 60647   773-235-3646

Chicago
Our Lady of Mercy
4432 N. Troy St.
Chicago, IL 60625   773-588-2620

Chicago
St. Pius V
1919 S. Ashland Ave.
Chicago, IL 60608   312-226-6161

Urban, Hispanic parish with large youth center; small Christian communities; powerful community organizing and economic development group that helps with needs including housing and day care.

Chicago
St. Agatha
3147 W. Douglas Blvd.
Chicago, IL 60623   773-522-3050

Chicago
St. Sabina
1210 W. 78th Place   773-483-4300
Chicago, IL 60620   www.saintsabina.org

Strong Bible-teaching ministry with an emphasis on praise and worship; large youth ministry; Thea Bowman Spiritual Advance Center (as opposed to a "retreat" center); pre-K-through-eighth-grade school; known for social justice programs, activism and street ministry.

Cicero
St. Anthony
1515 S. 50 Ave.
Cicero, IL 60650   708-652-0231

Downers Grove
St. Joseph
4824 Highland Ave.
Downers Grove, IL 60515   630-964-0216

Program to move gospel to workplace; youth ministry; school; religious education for handicapped children.

Evanston

St. Nicholas
806 Ridge Ave.
Evanston, IL 60202

847-864-1185
www.nickchurch.org

Multicultural church with strong outreach and peace and justice programs; newly renovated worship space in-the-round; welcoming all is a priority.

Iliopolis

Tri-parish Life Coordinators
PO Box 47
Iliopolis, IL 62539

217-486-3851

Rural cluster of three parishes without a resident priest; run by woman religious.

Inverness

Holy Family
2515 Palatine Rd.
Inverness, IL 60067

847-359 0042
www.holyfamilyparish.org

See parish profile, pp. 57–72.

Naperville

St. Margaret Mary
1450 Green Trails Dr.
Naperville, IL 60540

630-369-0777
www.smmp.com

Welcoming church where good preaching is the norm; full-time minister of justice and outreach; religious education for all ages.

O'Fallon

St. Nicholas
625 St. Nicholas Dr.
O'Fallon, IL 62269

618-632-1997

Parishioners focus on strengthening one another's faith; many youth programs with wide participation; men's faith group; Yesterday's Kids for senior volunteers; parenting classes; young mothers ministry.

INDIANA
Chesterton
St. Patrick
638 N. Calumet Rd.
Chesterton, IN 46304   219-926-1282
                     www.duneland.com/churches/stpats.htm

Encourages members to bring Christ to the workplace; open
to change; encourages lay involvement; Elizabeth ministry
(women who help new mothers); ministries to nursing
homes and shut-ins.

East Chicago
St. Patrick
3810 Grand Blvd.   219-398-1036
East Chicago, IN 46312   www.st-patrick-ec-in.org

Multicultural parish with welcoming attitude.

Evansville
St. Mary
613 Cherry St.
Evansville, IN 47713   812-425-1577

Downtown church reaches out to poor; strong on hospitality; dynamic liturgy; involved laypeople.

Evansville
Good Shepherd
2301 N. Stockwell Rd.
Evansville, IN 47715   812-477-5405

Stewardship parish with tuition-free schooling for parishioners
K–12; Helping Hands program, Over-fifties and social support
group address needs of parish members.

Merrillville
St. Joan of Arc
200 78th Ave.
Merrillville, IN 46410   219-769-1973

Welcoming parish that encourages lay involvement; collaborative leadership; prayerful liturgies.

Schererville

ST. MICHAEL
1 W. Wilhelm St.
Schererville, IN 46375   219-322-4505

Eucharist-centered; excellent music; homilies relevant to people's lives.

Valparaiso

ST. ELIZABETH ANN SETON
509 W. Division Rd.
Valparaiso, IN 46385   219-464-1624

IOWA
Bettendorf

ST. JOHN VIANNEY
4097 18th St.   319-332-7910
Bettendorf, IA 52722   www.sjvparish.org

Welcoming and accessible parish; collaborative leadership; excellent liturgy and music ministry; strong youth ministry; hospital visitation; ministry to sick and homebound.

Des Moines

BASILICA OF ST. JOHN
1915 University Ave.
Des Moines, IA 50314   515-244-3101

Neola

ST. PATRICK
308 4th St.
Neola, IA 51559   712-485-2124

Sioux City

BLESSED SACRAMENT
3012 Jackson St.
Sioux City, IA 51104   712-277-2949

Active parish known for peace-and-justice committee work for social and legislative change.

West Des Moines
SACRED HEART
1627 Grand Ave.
West Des Moines, IA 50265   515-225-6414

KANSAS
Garden City
OUR LADY, QUEEN OF ALL SAINTS
509 St. John St.
Garden City, KS 67846   316-275-4204

School; Stephen ministry (trained volunteers help those in stressful situations); Emmaus House.

Hays
ST. JOSEPH
215 W. 13th St.
Hays, KS 67601   785-625-7356

Teen Connection youth program; pastor hosts radio show for teens; ministry to the homebound; support group for singles/divorced; parish school.

Haysville
ST. CECILIA
1802 W. Grand
Haysville, KS 67060

Lakin
ST. ANTHONY
600 Soderberg
Lakin, KS 67860   316-355-6405

Spirit of togetherness; grade-school children can serve as lectors; good ecumenical cooperation.

Newton
ST. MARY
106 E. Eighth
Newton, KS 67114   316-282-0459
www.catholic-forum.com/stmarynewton/

Pratt
SACRED HEART
332 N. Oak St.
Pratt, KS 67124   316-672-6352
                  www.socencom.net/~ptc/sacred/parish.html

Emphasizes social justice and ecoawareness; high degree of
lay involvement; strong religious education for all ages.

Wichita
ST. FRANCIS OF ASSISI
861 N. Socora
Wichita, KS 67212   316-722-4404

See parish profile, pp. 109–127.

Wichita
ST. ELIZABETH ANN SETON
645 N. 119th St. W.   316-721-1686
Wichita, KS 67235   www.stfranciswichita.com

Stewardship parish with welcoming atmosphere; strong and
fast-growing RCIA program.

KENTUCKY
Anchorage
EPIPHANY
914 Old Harrods Creek Rd.
Anchorage, KY 40223   502-245-9733

Strong social justice and liturgical base.

Jeffersontown
ST. MICHAEL
12707 Taylorsville Rd.   502-266-5611
Jeffersontown, KY 40299   www.stmichaelchurch.org

Welcoming parish has "Super Greeters" at every Mass;
Lifelong Learning Center; outreach ministries; small
Christian communities.

Louisville

MOTHER OF GOOD COUNSEL
8509 Westport Rd.
Louisville, KY 40242-3099   502-425-2210

Strong RCIA and sacramental program; vacation Bible
school; bereavement care; music ministry.

LOUISIANA
Baton Rouge

IMMACULATE CONCEPTION
PO Box 74273
Baton Rouge, LA 70874   225-775-7062

African American parish has strong music program with
gospel and traditional choirs; food pantry; guest speakers;
spirit of lay ownership.

Lafayette

IMMACULATE HEART OF MARY
818 12th St.
Lafayette, LA 70501   337-235-4618

Metairie

ST. EDWARD THE CONFESSOR
4921 W. Metairie Ave.
Metairie, LA 70001   504-888-0703
Strong Life Teen program.

Metairie

ST. CLEMENT OF ROME
4317 Richland Ave.
Metairie, LA 70002   504-887-7821
                    www.catholic-church.org/stclementofrome/

Strong Life Teen program; vibrant music ministry.

New Orleans

ST. GABRIEL THE ARCHANGEL
4700 Pineda St.   504-282-0296
New Orleans, LA 70126-3599   www.stgabe.net

Multiracial parish provides partial tuition funding for master's degree in theological education for parishioners in return for ministry work.

New Orleans
ST. PETER CLAVER
1923 St. Philip St.
New Orleans, LA 70116-2199   504-822-8059

See parish profile, pp. 73–91.

New Orleans
ST. RAYMOND
3738 Paris Ave.   504-288-1272
New Orleans, LA 70122   www.josephite.com/parish/la/sr

New Orleans
ST. MONICA
2327 Galvez St.
New Orleans, LA 70125   504-821-9500

Opelousas
HOLY GHOST
788 N. Union St.
Opelousas, LA 70570   318-942-2732

MAINE
Brunswick
ST. CHARLES BORROMEO
132 McKeen St.   207-725-2624
Brunswick, ME 04011   www.saintcharlesbrunswick.org

Relevant homilies in a family-oriented parish; active social justice and peace commission supports Habitat for Humanity, hunger prevention, homeless shelters and more; young families actively involved with Sunday liturgies for children; family groups promote sense of community.

MARYLAND
Baltimore
CATHOLIC COMMUNITY OF ST. MICHAEL AND ST. PATRICK
7 S. Wolf St.
Baltimore, MD 21231   410-276-1646
    www.archbalt.org/parishes/urban/harboreast/michael
patrick.htm

Masses in Spanish and English; social outreach ministries.

Baltimore
ST. EDWARD
901 Poplar Grove St.
Baltimore, MD 21216   410-362-2000
    www.archbalt.org/parishes/urban/metrowest/edward.htm

Pastor encourages lay leadership; strong music program; fifteen youth groups; eleven basketball teams; emphasis on participation, discipleship and enthusiasm.

Columbia
ST. JOHN THE EVANGELIST
10431 Twin Rivers Rd.   410-964-1425
Columbia, MD 21044   www.sjerc.org

Ministry to prepare homeless for independent living; One Time Only program for volunteers to sample ministries and projects; multiple outreach and service ministries.

Derwood
ST. FRANCIS OF ASSISI
6701 Muncaster Rd.   301-840-1407
Derwood, MD 20855   www.stfrancisderwood.org

Multiethnic church; Sunday youth Mass with high teen involvement; student-friendly religious education; summer work camps for teens.

Gaithersburg
ST. ROSE OF LIMA
11701 Clopper Rd.   301-948-7545
Gaithersburg, MD 20878   www.rc.net/washington/st_rose

Suburban parish has Tagalog and Filipino masses; emphasis on hospitality and community; faith formation for all ages.

Silver Spring

St. Camillus
1600 St. Camillus Dr.
Silver Spring, MD 20903   301-434-8400
                    www.rc.net/washington/st_camillus/

Strong music programs; small faith groups; ministries to the sick and hurting; high lay involvement in social justice programs; religious education for English- and Spanish-speaking youth; child care; grade school; after-school tutoring.

MASSACHUSETTS
Chelsea

St. Rose of Lima
601 Broadway
Chelsea, MA 02150   617-889-2774

Lawrence

St. Mary's-Immaculate Conception
205 Hampshire St.
Lawrence, MA 01841   978-685-1111

This 151-year-old urban parish has learned to adapt to a changing city; stays focused on vision of unity; great lay participation in all aspects of parish life.

Milford

St. Mary of the Assumption
27 Pearl St.   508-473-2000
Milford, MA 01757   www.kersur.net/~frmika

Masses in Portuguese and English. Several choirs; Haitian ministry; outreach programs.

Newton

Our Lady Help of Christians
573 Washington St.   617-527-7560
Newton, MA 02458-1494   www.ourladys.com

See parish profile, pp. 1–18.

Roslindale

SACRED HEART
169 Cummins Hwy.   617-325-3322
Roslindale, MA 02131   www.sh-roslindale.org

Masses in English and Spanish; Adult, Spanish and youth choirs; charismatic prayer group.

Whitinsville

ST. PATRICK
7 East St.
Whitinsville, MA 01588   508-234-5656

Strong commitment to music and liturgy; children's Liturgy of the Word; preschool programs; nongraded approach to sacramental preparation; collaborative parish life; recently renovated one-hundred-year-old Romanesque Gothic church.

MICHIGAN
Ann Arbor

ST. FRANCIS OF ASSISI
2150 Frieze   734-769-2550
Ann Arbor, MI 48104   www.rc.net/lansing/st_fran

Emphasizes social justice and community outreach; Neighbor Works program helps welfare-to-work families; counseling service; small faith-sharing groups; singles ministry active in service projects; classes on spirituality and theology; family religious education.

Ann Arbor

ST. MARY STUDENT PARISH
331 Thompson   734-663-0557
Ann Arbor, MI 48104   www.umich.edu/~stmarys/

Family ministry with parents as catechists; strong RCIA; social justice emphasis; serves University of Michigan students.

Birmingham

St. Columban
1775 E. Melton Rd.
Birmingham, MI 48009   248-646-5224

Spontaneous prayers of faithful during Mass; collaborative
spirit between leadership and laypeople; emphasis on learning and personal development; suicide support group.

Carrollton

St. John the Baptist
3160 Carla Dr.   517-753-5103
Carrollton, MI 48604   stjohnthebaptist.catholicweb.com

Woman religious is pastoral administrator; Befriender ministry.

Clarkston

St. Daniel
7010 Valley Park Drive   248-625-4580
Clarkston, MI 48346   www.ring.com/stdan/stdan.htm

High level of participation; collaborative leadership; focus on
making community; continually strives for improvement.

Gaylord

St. Mary's Cathedral
606 N. Ohio Ave.
Gaylord, MI 49735   517-732-5448

Mt. Pleasant

St. Mary's University Parish
1405 S. Washington St.   517-773-3931
Mt. Pleasant, MI 48858   www.rc.net/saginaw/stmarycmu/

Faith and Profession groups have adult volunteers in various
professions meet with students to help meld ideas of work
and faith.

Saginaw

ST. MARY CATHEDRAL
615 Hoyt Ave.   517-752-8119
Saginaw, MI 48607   www.rc.net./saginaw/smc

A diverse and welcoming urban congregation; stress on stewardship, social action, justice and advocacy.

Ypsilanti

ST. JOSEPH
9425 Whittaker Rd.
Ypsilanti, MI 48197   734-461-6555

Friendly parish that serves a diverse congregation.

MINNESOTA
Bemidji

ST. PHILIP
710 Beltrami Ave.
Bemidji, MN 56601   218-751-4252

Stewardship parish; school has conflict management/media literacy program; thriving Life Teen Program and Mass.

Benson

ST. FRANCIS
508 13th St. N.
Benson, MN 56215   320-842-4271
            www.catholicareaparishes.org/stfrancisframe.htm

See parish profile, pp. 39–55.

Blaine

ST. TIMOTHY
707 89th Ave. NE
Blaine, MN 55434   612-784-1329
Strong pastoral outreach; Stephen Ministry; emphasis on faith formation; participative liturgy; many volunteer opportunities.

Clontarf

St. Malachy
PO Box 218
Clontarf, MN 56226   320-843-2026
www.catholicareaparishes.org/stmalachyframe.htm

See parish profile, pp. 39–55.

Danvers

Visitation
PO Box 18
Danvers, MN 56231   320-567-2278
www.catholicareaparishes.org/visitationframe.htm

See parish profile, pp. 39–55.

DeGraff

St. Bridget
501 3rd St. S.
De Graff, MN 56271   320-843-3883
www.catholicareaparishes.org/stbridgetframe.htm

See parish profile, pp. 39–55.

Eden Prairie

Pax Christi
12100 Pioneer Trail   612-941-3150
Eden Prairie, MN 55347   www.paxchristi.com

More than five thousand attend weekend Masses; strong
liturgy and community prayer; Christian life enrichment
ministries; staff on call twenty-four hours a day; nonprofit
Leaven Center develops people, programs and parishes.

Melrose

St. Mary
211 S. 5th Ave. E.
Melrose, MN 56352   320-256-4207

Rural parish with strong core groups in the liturgical ministries; good parental involvement in school; active pastoral
council; parishioners are mostly of German descent.

Minneapolis

St. Olaf
215 S. Eighth St.   612-332-7471
Minneapolis, MN 55402   www.saintolaf.org

Generation Cross television show for Generation Xers; retreats
four times per year; Faith & Work breakfast series with
nationally known speakers; urban church is accessible
through skyway.

Minneapolis

St. Stephen
2211 Clinton Ave. S.
Minneapolis, MN 55404   612-874-0311

Masses in Spanish and English; ministry for adults with special mental and physical needs; strong social justice and outreach programs, including shelter for homeless men and
residence for Native American women recovering from
chemical dependency; ministry to eight nursing homes.

Minneapolis

St. Joan of Arc
4537 3rd Ave. S.   612-823-8205
Minneapolis, MN 55417   www.stjoan.com

Liturgies often have guest speakers; strong music program;
welcome speaker starts each Mass.

Murdock

Sacred Heart
201 Orleans St.
Murdock, MN 56271   320-875-2451
            www.catholicareaparishes.org/sacredheartframe.htm

See parish profile, pp. 39–55.

MISSISSIPPI
Biloxi
CATHEDRAL OF THE NATIVITY OF THE BLESSED VIRGIN MARY
870 Howard Ave.
Biloxi, MS 39530   228-374-1717
                biloxidiocese.org/churchlist/biloxi_bvm.htm

MISSOURI
Chesterfield
INCARNATE WORD
13416 Olive Blvd.
Chesterfield, MO 63017   314-576-5366
    www.catholic-forum.com/churches/134iw/iw_home.html

Strong Life Teen program; Marriage Encounter; retreats;
strong music program.

Creve Coeur
ST. MONICA
12136 Olive Blvd.
Creve Coeur, MO 63141   313-434-4211
            www.catholic-forum.com/churches/205stmonica

Suburban stewardship parish with tuition-free, award-
winning school; six choirs; children's liturgies.

Kansas City
ST. THERESE LITTLE FLOWER
5814 Euclid Ave.
Kansas City, MO 64130   816-444-5406

Church community organization works to make church neighborhood safer; emergency assistance program; prayerful and
welcoming Sunday liturgies; gospel choir.

Springfield
SACRED HEART
1609 N. Summit
Springfield, MO 65803   417-869-3646

Redesigned church for modern liturgies; strong outreach to
community; diverse membership.

St. Louis
St. Alphonsus Liguori "Rock" Church
1118 N. Grand Blvd.   314-533-0304
St. Louis, MO 63106   www.stalphonsusrock.org

Dynamic liturgy in African American tradition; involved in parish neighborhood.

St. Louis
St. Francis Xavier College Church
3628 Lindell Blvd.   314-977-7300
St. Louis, MO 63108   www.slu.edu/departments/church

Excellent liturgies and music; diverse congregation includes all ages.

St. Louis
Most Precious Blood
3635 Union Rd.
St. Louis, MO 63125   314-487-6456
                    www.catholic-forum.com/churches/319mpb

Emphasizes daily Christian living; practical homilies; development of lay leadership; collaborative leadership.

MONTANA
Helena
St. Mary
1700 Missoula
Helena, MT 59601   406-442-5268

Effective lay pastoral leadership; solid liturgy.

NEBRASKA
Beemer
Holy Cross
517 N. Frasier
Beemer, NE 68716   402-528-3475
                    www.oarch.org/parishes/nebraska/beemer.html

Grand Island
St. Mary's Cathedral
Box 936
Grand Island, NE 68802   308-384-2523

Kearney
St. James
3801 Ave. A
Kearney, NE 68847   308-234-5536

Active parish known for strong liturgy; active youth ministry; helps with Habitat for Humanity.

Omaha
Sacred Heart
2218 Binney St.
Omaha, NE 68110   402-451-5755
www.oarch.org/parishes/omaha/sacred.html

Strong, innovative inner-city school; famed Freedom Choir; multicultural parish; sign language interpreters.

Stapleton
St. John
Box 309
Stapleton, NE 69163   308-636-2421

NEVADA
Las Vegas
Christ the King
4925 S. Torrey Pines
Las Vegas, NV 89118   702-871-1904
www.lvrj.com/communitylink/christtheking

Strong youth ministry; family-based religious education; outreach ministry; strong sense of community.

NEW JERSEY
Brant Beach

St. Francis of Assisi
4700 Long Beach Blvd.   609-494-8813
Brant Beach, NJ 08008   lbinet.com/nonprof/stfrancis.htm

Camden

St. Joseph Pro-Cathedral
2907 Federal St.   856-964-2776
Camden, NJ 08105   www.rc.net/camden/stjoseph

Strong parochial education; rehabilitates and sells abandoned
houses to first-time homeowners; runs urban retreat center
for lay ministry training.

Colts Neck

St. Mary
Rt. 34 and Phalanx Rd.
Colts Neck, NJ 07722   732-780-2666

Orientation for new members who are asked to sign a
covenant; support groups; bereavement ministry; retreats.

Gibbsboro

St. Andrew the Apostle
120 United States Ave.
Gibbsboro, NJ 08026   856-784-3878

Hoboken

Sts. Peter and Paul
404 Hudson St.   202-659-2276
Hoboken, NJ 07030   www.spphoboken.com

Urban parish with strong RENEW 2000 program; Catholic
Young Adults of Hoboken (CYAH) has spiritual and community outreach and social activities for ages twenty-one through
twenty-nine; youth Mass on Sunday nights.

Jersey City
St. Mary
209 Third St.
Jersey City, NJ 07302   201-653-3333

Livingston
St. Philomena
382 S. Livingston Ave.   973-992-0994
Livingston, NJ 07039   www.stphilomena.org

Cursillo weekend retreats; 25-plus singles group; youth ministry.

Newark
St. Rose of Lima
11 Gray St.
Newark, NJ 07107   201-482-0682
            www.newcommunity.org/strose/parish/index.html

Extensive social ministries include parish-run nursing home
and credit union; parish has built housing for more than five
thousand and turned former church into offices and restaurants.

Newark
Blessed Sacrament
15 Van Ness Place
Newark, NJ 07108   973-824 6548

Growing, predominantly African American church; strong
bereavement ministry; spirit-lifting gospel choirs; RCIA with
mandate to become involved in ministry.

North Caldwell
Notre Dame
358 Central Ave.
North Caldwell, NJ 07006   973-226-0979

Emphasizes Christian community through small faith-sharing
groups and Cornerstone spiritual renewal program; active
parishioner involvement in liturgical ministries.

Pompton Lakes

St. Mary
17 Pompton Ave.   973-835-0374
Pompton Lakes, NJ 07442   www.stmarys-pompton.org

Counseling services with fees based on ability to pay; family breakfasts held monthly; help for battered women; perpetual adoration.

Roseland

Our Lady of the Blessed Sacrament
28 Livingston Ave.   973-226-7288
Roseland, NJ 07068   www.olbs.org

Youth program; three choirs; social concerns committee.

Toms River

St. Joseph
509 Hooper Ave.
Toms River, NJ 08753   732-349-0018
                    www.angelfire.com/nj/cygnus/index.html

Upper Saddle River

Church of the Presentation
271 West Saddle River Rd.
Upper Saddle River, NJ 07458   201-327-1313
                    www.churchofpresentation.org

Innovative, thoughtful liturgy; Cornerstone weekend retreats; 20s and 30s ministry; soup kitchen ministry; funeral preparation and reception.

Westfield

St. Helen
1600 Rahway Ave.   908-232-1214
Westfield, NJ 07090   www.westfieldnj.com/sthelens

Suburban parish has Cornerstone retreats; creative parish religious education program includes all ages; strong, varied outreach ministries administered by lay committees.

NEW MEXICO
Albuquerque
SAN JOSE
2401 Broadway SE
Albuquerque, NM 87102   505-242-3658

Las Cruces
IMMACULATE HEART OF MARY CATHEDRAL
1240 S. Espina
Las Cruces, NM 88001   505-524-8563

High lay involvement; parish has Masses in Spanish and
English; strong Life Teen program.

Las Cruces
HOLY CROSS
1327 N. Miranda
Las Cruces, NM 88005
505-523-0167   www.holycrossparish.org

Strong parental leadership in parochial school and Life Teen
program; Spanish and English Masses; volunteer program;
outreach to shut-in elderly; parish nurse program.

Ranchos de Taos
SAN FRANCISCO DE ASIS
PO Box 72   505-758-2754
Ranchos de Taos, NM 87557   laplaza.org/~rubymtz

High lay involvement; Masses in English and Spanish.

Santa Fe
SANTA MARIA DE LA PAZ
11 College Ave.   505-473-4200
Santa Fe, NM 87505   www.smdlp.org

Life Teen; various support groups; monthly healing Masses;
artfully designed worship space.

NEW YORK
Albany

St. Vincent De Paul
900 Madison Ave.
Albany, NY 12208   518-489-5408

Creative, multiple ministries; imaginative use of building spaces.

Albany

St. John/St. Ann
157 Franklin St.   518-472-9091
Albany, NY 12202   www.sjsa.net

Serves inner-city neighborhood with hot meal twice weekly at the welcome table; furniture program distributes to needy; inclusive community; evangelization program.

Brooklyn

Transfiguration
263 Marcy Ave.
Brooklyn, NY 11211   718-388-8773
www.expage.com/page/transfiguration

Clifton Springs

St. Francis
12 Hibbard Ave.
Clifton Springs, NY 14432   315-462-2961
www.massintransit.com/ny/felixfrancis1-ny

Lay involvement encouraged; efforts to move the gospel into the workplace; hospitable parish.

East Islip

St. Mary
20 Harrison Ave.
East Islip, NY 11730   631-581-4266

Suburban with large school; Family Faith ministry attends to formation of family as unit; social ministry with much lay involvement.

Farmingdale

St. Kilian
485 Conklin St.   516-249-0127
Farmingdale, NY 11735   www.stkilian.com

Comprehensive ministry of consolation/bereavement with support group; personalized attention and education for parents prior to baptism of infants; social ministry/outreach has high lay participation.

Grafton

St. John Francis Regis
31 Owen Rd.
Grafton, NY 12082   518-279-4943

Small, rural parish with large number of young families; high involvement; program for young moms; solid religious education; family activities; active music ministry.

Holbrook

Good Shepherd
1370 Grundy Ave.   631-588-7689
Holbrook, NY 11741   good.shepherd.tripod.com

Emphasizes lay ministry; consolation ministry; RCIA; small church communities.

Interlaken

St. Francis Solanus
c/o Holy Cross Rectory
PO Box 1
Interlaken, NY 14847   607-532-8337

Loudonville

St. Pius X
2 Fairview Rd.
Loudonville, NY 12211   518-462-1336

Strong social justice efforts; bereavement ministry; involved in public policy issues; school; strong youth ministry.

New York

St. Francis Xavier
55 West 15th St.   212-627-2100
New York, NY 10011   www.rc.net/newyork/stfrancisxavier

Homeless shelter; Welcome Table serves one thousand meals
each Sunday; Christians in Recovery group; young singles;
small church communities.

New York

St. Malachy
239 W. 49th St.
New York, NY 10019   212-489-1340

Known as the "Actors' Chapel"; high lay participation, especially in liturgy; strong choir; diverse congregation includes
local residents, tourists, theatre folk and business people who
work in area.

New York

Our Lady of Guadalupe
229 W. 14th St.
New York, NY 10011   212-243-5317

Historically Hispanic parish with ministry to shut-ins; sacramental preparation; youth prayer group.

New York

St. Jude
431 W. 204th St.
New York, NY 10034   212-569-3000

New York

St. Ignatius Loyola
980 Park Ave.
New York, NY 10028   212-288-3588

Parish holds a variety of concerts and parish retreats; inter-
parish program for after-school religious education.

New York
St. Joseph's Chapel
385 South End Ave.
New York, NY 10280   212-466-0131

Strong adult education program.

New York
St. Mary
28 Attorney St.
New York, NY 10002   212-674-3266

Largely Hispanic parish; lay leadership emphasized through
various ministry programs; small faith-sharing groups; Spanish
Masses.

Penfield
St. Joseph
43 Gebhardt Rd.   716-586-8089
Penfield, NY 14526   www.frontiernet.net/~stjoseph

Strong faith-formation programs; jail ministry; workfare
assistance.

Penn Yan
St. Michael
214 Keuka St.
Penn Yan, NY 14527   315-536-7459

Plattsburgh
St. Peter
114 Cornelia St.   518-563-1692
Plattsburgh, NY 12901   www.saintpeterschurch.org

Soup kitchen; strong music ministry and preaching; emphasis on
baptism; strong Sunday morning religious education programs.

Rochester
St. Mary
15 St. Mary's Place   716-232-7140
Rochester, NY 14607   www.frontiernet.net/~stmary

Ministries to business/corporate community; strong music
programs; various social ministries to city area; good lay
involvement.

Westbury
ST. BRIGID
50 Post Ave.
Westbury, NY 11590   516-334-0021

Liturgy and religious education focused on family; RCIA.

NORTH CAROLINA
Charlotte
ST. GABRIEL
3016 Providence Rd.   704-364-5431
Charlotte, NC 28211   saintgabriel.catholicweb.com

Strong music program; varied support groups; strong on stewardship.

Raleigh
ST. RAPHAEL
5801 Falls of the Neuse Rd.   919-878-8499
Raleigh, NC 27609   www.saintraphael.org

Large suburban parish with well-planned liturgies; trained catechists for children's faith formation; health care ministry; AIDS care teams; much direct social ministry.

Raleigh
ST. FRANCIS OF ASSISI
11401 Leesville Rd.   919-847-8205
Raleigh, NC 27613   www.stfrancisraleigh.org

Large parish with lively worship and abundant programs; numerous opportunities for outreach and service; small communities; migrant ministry; Consolation & Care; young adult ministry.

Winston-Salem
HOLY FAMILY
4820 Kinnamon Rd.
Winston-Salem, NC 27103   336-778-0600

Promotes one-on-one evangelism with estranged Catholics; seasonal social ministries; assistance to local Hispanic community; emphasis on music.

OHIO
Chagrin Falls
St. Joan of Arc
496 East Washington St.   440-247-7183
Chagrin Falls, OH 44022-2999   www.stjoanofarc.org

Parish has full-time ministers for liturgy and music and for ministries to sick and bereaved; wellness program; strong RCIA and formation; day school for 240 children.

Cincinnati
Community of the Good Shepherd
8815 E. Kemper Rd.   513-489-8815
Cincinnati, OH 45249   www.good-shepherd.org

Youth group with service opportunities; wellness programs, large children's religious education program and summer Bible school; reflective prayer group; Bible study classes; several outreach programs; parish involves members in decisions affecting parish.

Cleveland
St. Malachi
2459 Washington Ave.   216-861-5343
Cleveland, OH 44113   www.stmalachi.org

St. Malachi is home to two distinct parishes that join in many projects; Malachi House provides care for the terminally ill; Malachi Mart offers low-cost shopping and is a fundraiser for other activities.

Cleveland
St. Peter
1533 E. 17th St.
Cleveland, OH 44114   216-861-1798

Cleveland

St. Agnes-Our Lady of Fatima
6800 Lexington Ave.
Cleveland, OH 44103   216-391-1655
www.cleveland.catholicnet.com/parish/stagnesourladyfatima

Dynamic African American parish with strong ministry for
and outreach to youth; joint programs with K–8 school and
new Family Center adjacent to church; small, but fast-growing church.

Columbus

Immaculate Conception
414 E. North Broadway   614-267-9241
Columbus, OH 43214   www.icramsnet.org

Adult renewal with yearly parish missions; outreach ministry; parish supports Habitat for Humanity; BREAD program (Building Respect, Equality and Dignity); ministry to
the sick; guest lecturers.

Dayton

St. James/Resurrection
130 Gramont Ave.
Dayton, OH 45417   937-228-7023

African American flavor to liturgy; two schools that stress both
academic and moral excellence; Catholic anchor in a changing
neighborhood; two parishes merged in a new church building.

Hudson

Saint Mary
340 N. Main St.
Hudson, OH 44236   330-653-8118

Life Teen; CAPS (Children of Aging Parents Support Group);
hunger task force; Habitat for Humanity; ministry of presence (grief support).

Kettering

Ascension
2025 Woodman Dr.   937-254-5411
Kettering, OH 45420   www.ascensionkettering.org

Comprehensive youth ministry; seminars for loved ones of inactive Catholics; children's Liturgy of the Word.

Lincoln Heights

ST. MARTIN DE PORRES
9927 Wayne Ave.
Lincoln Heights, OH 45215   513-554-4010

Strong youth participation in liturgies; African dance and drumming training; teaches youth traditional African American Christian values; weekly adult Bible studies.

Litchfield

OUR LADY HELP OF CHRISTIANS
9608 Norwalk Rd.   330-722-1180
Litchfield, OH 44253   www.dioceseofcleveland.org/ladyc/

One parish with six worship sites administered by three priests and three pastoral ministers; small-base Christian communities; youth ministry.

Martin

OUR LADY OF MT. CARMEL
1105 Elliston Rd.
Martin, OH 43445   419-836-7681

Small rural church; evenings for married couples with catered meal, speaker and renewal of vows; creative religious education; strong support of local soup kitchen.

Toledo

CORPUS CHRISTI UNIVERSITY PARISH
2955 Dorr St.   419-531-4992
Toledo, OH 43607   www.ccup.org/

Strong sense of commitment and community; labyrinth meditations; extended learning; lecture series; leadership training with scholarships for University of Toledo students; parish sponsors chair in Catholic studies.

OKLAHOMA
Edmond
St. John the Baptist
900 S. Littler St.   405-340-0691
Edmond, OK 73083   www.stjohn-catholic.org

Spirited, dynamic liturgies; high participation in worship, ministries and singing; outreach and evangelization to inactive Catholics through Journey of Faith program; many and active small Christian communities.

Oklahoma City
Epiphany
7336 West Britton Rd.   405-722-2110
Oklahoma City, OK 73132   www.theshop.net/epiphany

Active youth group with retreats, service projects and social functions; two choirs; Epiphany Classics (over-fifty-five group).

OREGON
Mt. Angel
St. Mary
575 E. College St.   503-845-2296
Mt. Angel, OR 97362   www.wstreetw.com/stmarys

Staffed by Benedictines; active and successful in community-wide outreach.

Oregon City
St. John the Apostle
417 Washington St.
Oregon City, OR 97045   503-656-3474

Emphasis on strong youth programs.

Portland
St. Andrew
4949 NE Ninth Ave.
Portland, OR 97211   503-281-4429

After-school tutoring; summer camp; small faith groups; strong music program; diverse mix of people; high lay involvement in social justice projects.

Portland
ST. FRANCIS OF ASSISI
330 SE 11th Ave.
Portland, OR 97214   503-232-5880

See parish profile, pp. 93–108.

St. Helen's
ST. FREDERIC
175 S. 13th St.   503-397-0148
St. Helen's, OR 97051   www.columbia-center.org/stfred/

Ecumenical programs; community involvement.

Woodburn
ST. LUKE
417 Harrison
Woodburn, OR 97071   503-981-5011

Diverse parish stresses inclusiveness and social responsibility.

PENNSYLVANIA
Erie
HOLY FAMILY
913 Fulton St.
Erie, PA 16503   814-452-4832

Clustered parish works to preserve traditions and devotions while encouraging needed changes and programs.

Hazleton
ST. GABRIEL
122 S. Wyoming St.
Hazleton, PA 18201   570-454-0212

Home to a large Spanish-speaking community; many programs to include all in parish life.

Huntingdon Valley

St. Albert the Great
212 Welsh Rd.
Huntingdon Valley, PA 19006   215-947-3500

Emphasizes stewardship and parishioner ownership of parish life through youth and young adult ministries, stewardship committee and parish school.

Lansdale

St. Stanislaus
51 Lansdale Ave.   215-855-3133
Lansdale, PA 19446   ststanislaus.com

A stewardship parish with some seventy organizations, including two full-time social ministers and five scripture study groups.

New Holland

Our Lady of Lourdes
737 Walnut St.
New Holland, PA 17557   717-354-2540

Philadelphia

St. William
6200 Rising Sun Ave.
Philadelphia, PA 19111   215-745-1389

Kindergarten and elementary school; outreach program to shut-ins and marginalized people; active senior citizen program.

Plymouth

St. John the Baptist
126 Nesbitt St.
Plymouth, PA 18651   570-779-9620

Shavertown

St. Therese
64 Davis St.
Shavertown, PA 18708   570-696-1144

Parish nursing program; health clinic; legal clinic staffed by professionals from the parish.

Wellsboro
ST. PETER
38 Central Ave.   570-724-3371
Wellsboro, PA 16901   www.catholic-church.org/st-peters

Samaritan House for terminally ill with twenty-four hour staffing by community volunteers; supports sister parish in Jamaica; funeral brunches; soup-kitchen visits; steady RCIA participation; shared wisdom process to make consensus decisions for parish.

RHODE ISLAND
Providence
ST. CHARLES BORROMEO
178 Dexter St.
Providence, RI 02907   401-421-6411

Charismatic renewal programs; weekly prayer program for children; perpetual eucharistic adoration.

Providence
ST. TERESA OF AVILA
18 Pope St.
Providence, RI 02907   401-831-7714

SOUTH CAROLINA
Charleston
CATHEDRAL OF ST. JOHN THE BAPTIST
120 Broad St.   803-724-8395
Charleston, SC 29401   www.charlestoncathedral.org

Growing urban parish; integrated school; strong liturgies and music.

Conway
ST. JAMES
1071 Academy Dr.   843-347-5168
Conway, SC 29526   members.aol.com/stjamessc

Hispanic ministry; efforts to oppose capital punishment;
ministry to death row inmates; extensive ministry to the
sick; bilingual RCIA; annual ministries fair (to acquaint
parishioners with volunteer options).

Mount Pleasant
CHRIST OUR KING
1122 Russell Dr.   843-884-5587
Mount Pleasant, SC 29464   www.christourking.org

Strong senior ministry, social outreach and music ministries;
works ecumenically for social action.

Ridgeland
ST. ANTHONY
700 Jacob Smart S.
Ridgeland, SC 29936   843-726-3606

Small rural parish with scripture and sacramental educational
programs for adults; prison ministry with weekly visits to
two local prisons and Mass in Spanish; high lay involvement.

Taylors
PRINCE OF PEACE
1209 Brushy Creek Rd.   864-268-4352
Taylors, SC 29687-4103   fp.scsn.net/pop/

Welcoming parish with multiple ministries, including spiritual direction, employment support group and counseling
group.

SOUTH DAKOTA
Sioux Falls
OUR LADY OF GUADALUPE
1220 E. 8th St.
Sioux Falls, SD 57103   605-338-8126

TENNESSEE
Memphis

St. Augustine
1169 Kerr Ave.
Memphis, TN 38106   901-774-2297
www.cdom.org/parishes/st%20augustine

Health ministry; award-winning African American choir
evangelizes through music; social action committee; SALT
(young adult group for spiritual and service activities).

Nashville

Cathedral of the Incarnation
2001 West End Ave.
Nashville, TN 37203   615-327-2330

Urban parish with strong and varied social outreach programs; built three hermitages for members to use for prayer
and solitude.

TEXAS
Austin

Sacred Heart
5909 Reicher Dr.
Austin, TX 78723   512-926-2552

Evangelism and visitation; multiethnic congregation; ministry
to the poor.

Austin

St. Thomas More
10205 Ranch Rd., 620 N.   512-258-1161
Austin, TX 78726   www.stmaustin.org

Life Teen; 50 percent of parish under eighteen years of age;
welcoming; high degree of lay involvement and empowerment.

Austin

St. Louis
7601 Burnet Rd.   512-454-0384
Austin, TX 78757   www.austindiocese.org/stlouisaustin

Large Hispanic and Anglo congregation; extensive social ministries; outstanding parochial school and family ministries; emphasis on stewardship, worship and spiritual life.

El Paso

St. Pius X
1050 North Clark Rd.   915-772-3226
El Paso, TX 79905   www.elpasoparishes.org/stpiusx.htm

See parish profile, pp. 19–38.

Ft. Worth

St. Bartholomew
3601 Altamesa Blvd.   817-292-7813
Ft. Worth, TX 76133   www.stbartsfw.org

Weekly adult Bible studies; share groups; large senior citizen volunteer group; active ministry to the sick.

Houston

St. Cecilia
11720 Joan of Arc
Houston, TX 77024   713-465-3414

Parish of 2,500 households; high degree of lay involvement; effective children's formation in liturgical prayer; well-baby clinic.

Houston

St. Anne
2140 Westheimer   713-526-3276
Houston, TX 77098   www.saintanne.org

Mixed Hispanic and Anglo parish; strong emphasis on marriage preparation and RCIA; large Hispanic youth ministry program.

Houston
St. Cyril of Alexandria
10503 Westheimer   713-789-1250
Houston, TX 77042   www.rc.net/galveston/st_cyril/

Masses in English and Spanish; participative liturgies; one
hundred faith-sharing groups; RCIA and adult faith formation
has full-time minister; religious education for all age groups.

Houston
St. Francis Xavier
4600 Reed Rd.   713-738-2311
Houston, TX 77051   www.cathworld.org/sfx

Active African American parish with youth ministry; Bible
study groups; charismatic prayer group.

Houston
St. Francis of Assisi
5102 Dabney St.
Houston, TX 77026   713-672-7773

Houston
St. Mary
3006 Rosedale St.
Houston, TX 77004   713-528-0571

Pasadena
St. Pius the Fifth
824 S. Main St.   713-473-9484
Pasadena, TX 77506   www.rc.net/galveston/st_pius/

Urban parish with spirit of openness to all; half of the Masses
are in Spanish; strong RCIA; mixed Hispanic and Anglo congregation.

San Antonio

SAN FERNANDO CATHEDRAL
115 Main Plaza   210-227-1297
San Antonio, TX 78205   www.sfcathedral.org/welcome.htm

Large, urban Hispanic parish strives for liturgies that speak to members in their language and culture; nationally broadcast bilingual Mass; intensive leadership development in ministries.

San Antonio

SAN JUAN DE LOS LAGOS
3231 El Paso St.
San Antonio, TX 78208   210-433-9722

Program for senior citizens makes a difference in this barrio parish; strong music program; welcoming atmosphere; vigorous religious education program and leaders.

San Antonio

HOLY ROSARY
159 Camino Santa Maria
San Antonio, TX 78228   210-433-3241

Thriving Christian education program; many adults involved in youth program.

San Antonio

ST. ROSE OF LIMA
9883 Marbach Rd.
San Antonio, TX 78245   210-675-1920
                  www.massintransit.com/tx/roselima-tx-sanan

Multicultural suburban church with strong religious education program; high degree of lay involvement in ministries; parish encourages members to know one another by name; RCIA tries to bring non-Catholic spouses to church.

San Antonio

ST. PAUL
350 Sutton Dr.
San Antonio, TX 78228   210-733-7152

Ministries for poor, elderly, sick, single parents, bereaved and homebound; youth programs; parish promotes ecumenical involvement in the community; English and Spanish Masses; full-time directors for youth, religious education, liturgy and social ministries.

VIRGINIA
Falls Church
St. Anthony of Padua
3305 Glen Carlyn Rd.   703-820-7111
Falls Church, VA 22041   www.stanthonyparish.org

Multicultural parish characterized by strong sense of community; all communications and celebrations bilingual; social outreach includes home for unwed mothers and health fairs; strong religious education program.

Richmond
Epiphany
11000 Smoketree Dr.   804-794-0222
Richmond, VA 23236   www.epiphanychurch.org

High parishioner involvement in liturgy ministry; mentoring program for students; single annual stewardship pledge; religious education for about fifteen hundred children and youth.

Richmond
St. Bridget
6006 Three Chopt Rd.   804-282-9511
Richmond, VA 23226   www.stbridgets.org

Social ministry focused on housing; strong community involvement in liturgical ministries; comprehensive youth programs; campus ministry to University of Richmond.

Richmond
St. Edward
2700 Dolfield Dr.   804-272-2948
Richmond, VA 23235   www.stedwardtheconfessor.com

Hospitable suburban parish with ministries to sick and homebound; homeless outreach; inclusive liturgy strives for relevancy.

Richmond
ST. MARY
9505 Gayton Rd.
Richmond, VA 23229   804-740-4044
                              www.saintmary.org/parish/index.html

Prison ministries for men and women inmates at nearby correctional facilities; ministers to five nursing homes.

Virginia Beach
HOLY SPIRIT
1396 Lynnhaven Pkwy.   757-468-3600
Virginia Beach, VA 23456-2798   www.holy-spirit-parish.org

Several social justice programs, including Spirit House for women, winter shelter for homeless, soup kitchen ministry and a planned Spirit House II for men; catechumenate for adults and children; this tithing parish emphasizes stewardship.

Virginia Beach
ASCENSION
4853 Princess Anne Rd.   757-495-1886
Virginia Beach, VA 23462   www.churchoftheascension.org

Winter shelter for homeless; singles group; Soup & Sacrament (evening meal, videos and liturgy on Tuesdays during Lent).

WASHINGTON
Connell
ST. VINCENT
Box 1030
Connell, WA 99326   509-234-2262

Pasco
ST. PATRICK
1320 W. Henry   509-547-8841
Pasco, WA 99301   www.rc.net/spokane/st_patrick

Multicultural parish with Masses in Spanish and English weekly and in Vietnamese monthly; holds regional

Evangelization Congress annually with speakers from United States and Latin America; strong religious education and youth ministry programs.

Seattle

ST. JAMES CATHEDRAL
804 Ninth Ave.   206-622-3559
Seattle, WA 98104   www.stjames-cathedral.org

Racially and socioeconomically diverse congregation; winter shelter program for homeless; soup kitchen; critically acclaimed music ministry; RCIA; many young single adults.

Seattle

ST. THERESE
3416 East Marion St.   206-325-2711
Seattle, WA 98112   www.sainttthereseparish.org

Multiracial congregation; contemporary and gospel masses.

Sunnyside

ST. JOSEPH
920 S. 6th St.
Sunnyside, WA 98944   509-837-2243
                           http://users.bentonrea.com/~stjoseph

Multicultural Masses; Life Teen; strong RCIA; two Spanish youth groups; grief and bereavement committee; small base communities in Spanish and English.

Walla Walla

ST. PATRICK
408 W. Poplar St.
Walla Walla, WA 99362   509-525-1602

Bilingual religious education for Anglo/Hispanic congregation; many ministries in Spanish, including sacramental preparation programs.

Yakima

St. Joseph
212 N. 4th St.
Yakima, WA 98901   509-248-1911

Primarily Mexican American congregation; outreach to the
poor and marginalized; education for Hispanic parents and
children; English and Spanish Masses.

WISCONSIN
Franklin

St. James
7219 S. 27th St.
Franklin, WI 53132   414-761-0486

Janesville

Nativity of Mary
313 E. Wall St.   608-752-7861
Janesville, WI 53545   www.nativitymary.org

Great liturgies; successful RCIA shares coordinator with
other parishes in city; strong lay leadership; lay-run Taize
prayer.

Kenosha

St. Mark
7117 14th Ave.   414-652-1972
Kenosha, WI 53143   www.stmark-kenosha.org

Large, well-organized parish with a Latin American Center
for Hispanic members; strong stewardship committee;
human concerns group addresses different outreach needs
each month.

Milwaukee

Our Lady of Lourdes
3722 S. 58th St.
Milwaukee, WI 53220   414-545-4316

Committed to prayerful, creative liturgy; family-based religious education and RCIA; laypeople feel empowered in ministries; energetic youth program; variety of small faith-sharing groups.

Racine

St. Patrick
1100 Erie St.
Racine, WI 53402   262-637-7619

Masses in Spanish and English; Thursday meal program for those in need; children's reading program; survival English/Spanish eight-week language study; dance lessons for all ages on Sunday afternoons build community; winter fund-raising dance.